Foreword

Thank you very much for choosing this book!

If you are looking for a compact practical guide for the great and versatile Raspberry Pi mini-PC, then you are in the right place and well advised with this book: "Raspberry Pi | 101"! I am an engineer (M.Eng.) and would like to introduce you to the Raspberry Pi in a simply explained way. In this book, you will learn theoretical background knowledge about the Raspberry Pi, as well as the practical application through great and exciting example projects. This book offers you an easy-to-understand, intuitively structured and practical introduction to the world of the mini-PC!

In this course, we deal together and step by step with the assembly of the Raspberry Pi board, the installation of the necessary software as well as with the programming and the creation of first projects, e.g., a motion detector system.

This basics book is especially for those who have no or only very primitive previous knowledge about Raspberry Pi. No matter what age you are, what profession you have, whether you are a pupil, student, or pensioner. This book is for everyone who is interested in the fascinating topics: Electronics, Raspberry Pi and Programming. So, in this Raspberry Pi basic course you will learn everything you need to know as a beginner about the world of the mini-PC, its construction, use, and background!

Table of contents

1 Introduction to the Raspberry Pi

1.1 What is a Raspberry Pi?

A Raspberry Pi is a kind of mini PC that consists of only one board with a processor and a few connectors. You can use it to perform basic functions, but most importantly to learn how to use computer technology, programming, and electronics. The Raspberry Pi Foundation has launched this single-board computer. This foundation is a non-profit organization founded in the United Kingdom whose goal is to teach people about computers and make computer education more accessible.

In 2012, the Raspberry Pi Foundation had launched its first Raspberry Pi model. The development of the Raspberry Pi has not stopped since then, and several updated versions and variants have been added to the product portfolio since then. The first Raspberry Pi model was quite modestly equipped with a 700 MHz single-core processor and 256 MB of RAM. The latest model consists of a quad-core CPU with a clock speed of over 1.5 GHz and 4 GB of RAM.

1.2 The Raspberry Foundation

It has a high value for our society that many companies have decided to develop modern resources for quality technical education of students. Especially at a young age, contact with the subjects: Computer technology, electronics, and programming essential for interest in the subject and skills for it. Raspberry Pi is one such organization that has recognized the current educational needs and provides a user-friendly and cost-effective solution for students and anyone else interested in technology. Raspberry Pi was originally launched in 2009 to promote computer science education in schools.

The Raspberry Pi Foundation's mission is to provide low-cost, yet powerful computers that individuals can use to learn how to solve technical problems while having fun doing it. This promotes awareness of the topic of computers and digitalization.

The organization was split into two halves in early 2013: the Raspberry Pi Foundation, which is mainly responsible for the educational aspect, and the Raspberry Pi Trading Ltd., which takes care of technology and trade. Proceeds from the sale of Raspberry Pi devices are used to fund the Foundation's charitable activities. Raspberry Pi Trading Ltd. is a (100%) subsidiary of the Raspberry Pi Foundation.

1.3 Hardware specifications of the Raspberry Pi

The Raspberry Pi is available in several models. The two most important ones with the most features are the models A and B. We will take a look at which other models are available and which model you should choose in the next chapter. The main difference between models A and B is the USB port. The Model A versions consume less power and do not have an Ethernet port (i.e., no LAN or Internet connection). The Model B boards, on the other hand, have an Ethernet port.

A standard Raspberry Pi board contains the following components:

- Memory (RAM)
- (Main) processor (CPU)
- Graphics processor (GPU)
- Ethernet connection
- GPIO interface
- Xbee socket (wireless communication)
- UART (serial interface)
- Connection for the power source

There are also a variety of ports for other external hardware. A storage medium is also required. A microSD memory card is used as a hard drive replacement in this case. The Pi board boots via the SD card in the same way as a PC that boots the operating system, e.g., Windows, from a built-in hard disk.

The basic hardware requirements of the Raspberry Pi board primarily include the aforementioned microSD-card with a Linux operating system, a keyboard, a monitor, a power supply and a video connection. Optional hardware specifications include a USB mouse, a USB hub with power supply, a case and an online connection (WLAN or LAN).

Working memory – RAM:

The RAM (Random Access Memory) of a Raspberry Pi varies depending on the model and version. The RAM of the current Raspberry Pi 4 board ranges from 512 MB to 4 GB.

System-on-a-Chip (SoC):

System-on-a-Chip (SoC) stands for a combination of CPU and GPU. The Raspberry Pi is powered by an ARM-11 CPU. A separate Broadcom CPU is used in each board. The Broadcom chips and their use are listed below.

- **BCM2835:** used in the Raspberry Pi 1 and Zero models
- **BCM2836:** Processor for the Raspberry Pi 2 generation
- **BCM2837:** Processor for the Raspberry Pi 3 generation
- **BCM2837B0:** Processor for the Raspberry Pi 3B+ and 3A+ generations
- **BCM2711:** Processor for the Raspberry Pi 4B generation

Storage capacity:

The Raspberry Pi uses an SD card that works like a hard disk. SD cards with a capacity of more than 256 GB can be used in the Plus models of the Raspberry Pi.

Display connector:

The HDMI port on the Raspberry Pi board allows connection to sophisticated HDMI displays. There is also an RCA connector for connecting to older computer monitors and TVs. There is no VGA port, but this is no longer in use with modern displays anyway.

Network connection:

The Raspberry Pi team also added a network adapter to the board that allows users to connect to the Internet. Some models have an Ethernet port for LAN connectivity, while others include a built-in Wi-Fi adapter that allows users to connect to a Wi-Fi connection. Some boards also have a Wi-Fi dongle option that enables a wireless network connection via a USB connection.

GPIO interface:

The main interface of the Raspberry Pi is **GPIO** (General Purpose Input/Output). GPIO pins are used to connect to electronic components such as LEDs, switches, and a variety of other devices. The user can perform Arduino operations (Arduino is also a single-board PC similar to the Raspberry Pi) using the GPIO pins, such as connecting sensors and retrieving information. The Raspberry Pi offers a graphical user interface compared to the Arduino.

Connection for the power source:

The board's power supply is ensured with the help of a micro-USB connector. The Raspberry Pi models A and B need – like many other single-board PCs – a 5 V voltage.

Camera connection:

You can connect a camera module to the Raspberry Pi via the camera port. Such a camera module must be purchased additionally.

UART interface:

The serial input and output is provided by the **UART** interface (Universal Asynchronous Receiver/Transmitter). This allows serial data to be sent as text, which is convenient for debugging code conversion.

Features of the Raspberry Pi Model A:

- 256 MB SD RAM memory
- Single 2.0 USB port
- Dual Core VideoCore IV multimedia coprocessor
- HDMI (1.3 & 1.4) Composite RCA video output
- 3.5 MM jack, HDMI, audio output
- SD, MMC, SDIO card slot for on-board memory
- Linux operating system
- Broadcom BCM2835 SoC full-HD multimedia processor
- Dimensions 8.6 cm x 5.4 cm x 1.5 cm

Features of the Raspberry Pi Model B:

- 512 MB SDRAM memory
- Single 2.0 USB port
- Dual Core VideoCore IV multimedia coprocessor
- HDMI (1.3 & 1.4) Composite RCA video output
- 3.5 MM jack, HDMI, audio output
- SD, MMC, SDIO card slot for on-board memory
- Linux operating system
- Integrated 10/100 Ethernet RJ45 jack
- Broadcom BCM2835 SoC full-HD multimedia processor
- Dimensions 8.6 cm x 5.4 cm x 1.7 cm

The Raspberry Pi is part of the open-source environment: it runs Linux (in several variants). The Raspberry Pi's main operating system is open-source and runs a number of open-source software. The Raspberry Pi Foundation works with the Linux kernel and many other open-source programs, and makes most of its software open-source.

2 Important Raspberry Pi models

The Raspberry Pi is a great device for understanding a computer, and at a price that is extremely affordable. The simplest models of a Raspberry Pi cost between $10 - $100. The circuit board of a Raspberry Pi is so small that it fits in the palm of your hand.

First released in 2012, the Raspberry Pi is in constant development. Over time, the company has produced a variety of single-board computers, all with the name Raspberry Pi and a model name. There are now a large number of variants and models.

Raspberry Pi boards are named after their design and generation. Models 1,2,3,4 of the Raspberry Pi Zero are the existing versions of the standard Raspberry Pi boards. Model A, Model A +, Model B and Model B + were the four original Raspberry 1 models. The original credit card sized format is represented by the B models. Since the newest A models have a smaller and more compact footprint, the networking capabilities here are generally limited. Zero versions are the smallest of all Raspberry boards, which affects their connectivity options. Zero versions are available with or without GPIO headers. Meanwhile, there is also the Raspberry Pi Pico, which is a very primitive version, and will therefore not be looked at in more detail here. It is already available for less than $10.

We will take a look at the models in the current latest generations below.

In addition to the models, there are also accessories such as "add-on boards", cameras, display, peripherals, connectors, and housings. The best overview can be found at: https://www.raspberrypi.com/products/

2.1 Raspberry Pi <u>4</u> Model <u>B</u> (2019)

You might wonder why we start with the model B here because there is also a model A. But we start here with the Model B because contrary to the alphabetical order, this was originally the first model series of the Raspberry Pi in 2012. Most of the components on the Raspberry Pi 4 Model B's board have been changed over time. These include: the processor, the memory, the USB ports, the HDMI output, the network port, and the power port. Meanwhile, we have arrived at generation 4.

The core design of the processor has been changed to a new, highly efficient and more powerful microarchitecture. The Raspberry Pi was changed from the Cortex-A53 processor (CPU) to the quad-core Cortex-A72 processor (CPU) with a total of four cores, with the introduction of this version of the Raspberry Pi.

This change allows the mini-PC to work much faster while consuming significantly less power.

In addition to the significant improvements to the CPU (main processor), the Pi team has also upgraded the GPU (graphics processor) of the

Raspberry Pi 4 Model B. The Raspberry Pi has been upgraded from the Broadcom VideoCore IV to the VideoCore VI as part of this update.

This new GPU brings some improvements that significantly increase efficiency and expand the possibilities. For example, this means that you can now use two 4K displays simultaneously with this Raspberry Pi model.

With the Raspberry Pi 4 Model B you can now also use more RAM than with the previous models. Since the Pi 2 Model B, the Raspberry Pi RAM was limited to 1 GB. With the Raspberry Pi 4, however, you now have a choice of 1, 2, 4 or 8 GB of RAM. The larger the working memory, the more expensive the price of the mini-PC, of course.

In addition, two of the total four USB 2.0 ports have been replaced by two USB 3.0 ports in the Raspberry Pi 4 Model B. The introduction of USB 3.0 is a significant step forward for everyone who needs fast data transfers.

As for the connectivity of the Raspberry Pi 4 Model B, the Wi-Fi module has not changed. However, the Bluetooth module has been upgraded from 4.2 LS BLE to 5.0. The team has also improved the Ethernet connection so that almost the full Gigabit speed of the port is reached.

The single HDMI port that has been present on all Raspberry models since launch has been replaced by two micro-HDMI ports on the Pi 4 Model B.

The last major change made to this generation of the Raspberry Pi was the change of the power connector. The models have used a micro-USB port for power since the first Raspberry Pi. However, with the Pi 4 Model B, the decision was made to use a USB-C port.

2.2 Raspberry Pi <u>3</u> Model <u>A+</u> (2018)

The original Raspberry Pi Model A was introduced in 2014. The Model A+ variants of the Raspberry Pi have seen a significant improvement in 2018.

The development team wanted to bring most of the improvements of the Raspberry Pi 3 Model B+ into the compact Model A layout. So, this variant has the same dimensions as the Raspberry Pi 1 Model A+, but with all the performance improvements of the 3 B+ version.

The Raspberry Pi 3 Model A+ has a similar quad-core ARM processor (CPU) as the B+ variant of the Raspberry. The clock speed of this processor is 1.4 GHz, just like the Pi 3 model B+.

Like the earlier models of the A+, this board only has a single USB port and no Ethernet interface. However, similar microchips as in the Pi 3 B+ have been used to improve the board's efficiency.

These new enhancements to the A+ board allow users to access both Bluetooth and Wi-Fi without using a USB dongle. Thanks to compatibility with the 2.4 GHz and 5 GHz frequency bands, the processor board can connect to most Wi-Fi networks.

The price of the A+ model was increased slightly with this version. However, the price increase was minimal compared to all the innovations implemented in this model.

2.3 Raspberry Pi Compute Module 4 (2020)

The Raspberry Pi Compute Module 4 was launched in 2020 and contains many of the advancements of the Raspberry Pi 4. The term Compute Module simply refers to a different design of the Raspberry Pi 4. It is a plug-in module for use as an "embedded system" in other computer systems. However, this module is rather intended for professional use and not suitable for beginners. Therefore, we will not go into more detail here.

2.4 Raspberry Pi <u>Zero</u> (2015)

The Raspberry Pi Zero is even smaller compared to the original models. The Raspberry Pi Zero is only half the size of a model A+, but still has many similar features.

This Raspberry Pi has the same microprocessor and RAM as a Raspberry Pi 1 Model B+. So, the Raspberry Pi Zero is equipped with a single-core ARM CPU processor and 512 MB RAM. While these features are not as impressive as the A and B variants, the Raspberry Pi Zero is available at a much lower price. The Raspberry Pi Zero model is available for under $10, which can be considered extremely cheap in this range.

The board has a single micro-USB port for power, a microSD card to replace a hard drive, and a small HDMI port for video output. The only component missing from this model is an Ethernet port. Because of the smaller size, this board allows you to use the power and diversity of a Raspberry Pi and all of its GPIO features in even smaller applications.

2.5 Raspberry Pi Zero <u>W</u> (2017)

The Raspberry Pi Zero W was announced in 2017 with the goal of maintaining the small footprint of the Raspberry Zero models while offering the same connectivity options – including the same connectivity – as the Raspberry Pi 3 Model B. This was achieved by adding Bluetooth (4.1 BLE) and Wi-Fi (b/g/n single-band 2.4GHz) to the board.

Before the introduction of these ports on the Raspberry Pi Zero, the user had to use a USB dongle for the connection.

However, with the Pi Zero W model series, the Raspberry Pi has not undergone any significant changes other than improving its connectivity. The functionality of the board is identical to that of the original. The power requirements have also remained unchanged.

The price of the device has increased slightly due to the installation of the new component. You should also only use this model if you need Wi-Fi or Bluetooth for your project, otherwise the previously presented Raspberry Pi Zero model can be used.

2.6 Raspberry Pi 400 (2020)

The Raspberry Pi 400 was released in 2020 and differs considerably from the shape of the Raspberry Pi computer series. As you can see, this model could also be mistaken for a keyboard. Basically, it was also actually just a Raspberry Pi integrated into a fully functional keyboard. Three advantages can easily be seen: a) you no longer need an additional keyboard, b) the Raspberry Pi and the ports are protected by a case c) the design is more tasteful.

The Raspberry Pi 400 has the same basic specifications as the Raspberry Pi 4 model. However, some things have been modified as well. For example, the Pi 400's processor has a higher clock speed than the base model 4. The Pi 400's clock speed has been increased from 1.5 GHz to 1.8 GHz. This means that you should notice a slight improvement in performance compared to the base model.

By the way, there is only one variant of the Pi 400 model with 4 GB RAM (working memory).

Another difference to the Raspberry Pi 4 is that the Pi 400 only has three USB ports. The first is a USB 2.0 port, the second, and third are each a USB 3.0 port. All other technical specifications of the device are similar to the Raspberry Pi 4. Available are the same GPIO pins, an Ethernet port as well as Wi-Fi and Bluetooth interfaces.

2.7 Which Raspberry Pi model is best for me?

When you think of a Raspberry Pi, you have a small, credit card-sized computer in mind that you can use just like a real PC for most common tasks, such as creating documents, surfing the web, and programming software. However, as we have just seen, there is not just one model, but several different models. How are you supposed to choose? Don't worry if you haven't been able to make a decision yet, the following points will help you choose the right Raspberry Pi for your project. One thing in advance: It mainly depends on the field of application and the usage requirements.

What are your requirements?

Before you can make a choice, you need to determine the requirements for the mini-PC. The first thing you should do is decide which specifications are most important for your project. As a rule, the requirements can be summarized with the following key points:

- The processing power of the system (speed of the CPU)
- The working memory of the system (software requirements?)
- The size and weight of the system (400, Model A, Zero?)
- The price you are willing to pay
- Whether the support of I/O is required
- Whether Wi-Fi or Bluetooth is required
- Which connections must be mandatory

Let's take a more detailed look at some of these requirements below.

Speed:

In the context of a computer, the speed of the processor is probably one of the most important aspects. Compared to other microcontrollers, the Raspberry Pi family of computers is quite fast, but there are still significant differences between the individual Raspberry Pi models.

For example, the Model B of the Raspberry Pi has a quad-core ARM Cortex processor, while the Model A, which was released immediately after the

Model B, only has a single-core 700MHz ARM processor. This means that the Model B is significantly faster than the Model A.

Random Access Memory (RAM):

Depending on whether you want to run complex applications in a computer system or not, the RAM can be a decisive criterion. The Raspberry Pi A model series has 256 MB to 512 MB of RAM, the Raspberry generations 2 and 3 of the B model series, on the other hand, already have 1 GB of RAM, which is shared by the CPU and GPU, i.e., the main processor and graphics processor. If memory is critical to you or your project, you should consider at least the Raspberry Pi Generation 3 B Series, if not the Raspberry Pi Generation 4 B Series, with either 1, 2, 4 or 8 GB of memory.

Size and weight:

This criterion is mostly not crucial, since all Raspberry Pi model series are already very compact and light anyway. However, a few applications may have even stricter requirements for size and weight. In such cases, the Raspberry Pi Compute model can be the clear winner. Besides the Compute module, which is rather not suitable for beginners, the Raspberry Pi Zero with its extremely compact form comes into question here. However, it has less RAM and computing power than other models. As the smallest variant, the Raspberry Pi Pico would also be available. However, this model series was not discussed in detail in the previous chapter, since it can rather be seen as a microcontroller, but not as a single-board PC. The RAM and processor are significantly smaller than in the other Raspberry Pi model series. You can't run an operating system like the Raspberry Pi OS or Linux on it either, but really only implement simple programming or electronics projects with it.

GPIO I/O:

Raspberry Pi computers are typically used when I/O pins are required, such as for connecting sensors or other components. Since the Raspberry Pi boards have GPIO pin connectors, the Raspberry Pi A and B are ideal for connecting to external devices. Surprisingly, the Raspberry Pi Zero, just like the B model, also has 17 GPIO, meaning you wouldn't have to sacrifice anything here if you decide to go with the smaller model line. However, we will come back to this topic in more detail in another chapter.

Connectivity:

The most important difference between the Raspberry Pi systems is their network capability. The two model series A and A+ of the first generation do not have network connectivity; the model series B in the first and second generation, on the other hand, have Ethernet ports. However, since people don't like to work with a cable in their way, built-in wireless interfaces for Bluetooth and Wi-Fi are more important, such as the latest model series of A and B, but also the Raspberry Pi Zero W (note: only with the addition "W") model has.

It is best to consider which model comes into question based on the previous points. However, you certainly won't go wrong with the Raspberry Pi 4 B or the somewhat cheaper Raspberry Pi Zero W! These are my recommendations.

2.8 Possible uses of Raspberry Pi computers

The Raspberry Pi is a credit card-sized computer that is compact, inexpensive and extremely powerful. This was developed to teach the basics of electronics and computer science to students and others, especially those in low-income regions. Countless school projects, circuits, robotics applications, automations, etc., have already been developed with the Raspberry Pi.

What can you specifically use a Raspberry Pi for? Below are some Raspberry Pi applications to give you some inspiration of what all is possible with such a primitive and small PC in the form of a circuit board.

Desktop PC: The simplest application of the Raspberry Pi is as a desktop computer. Besides the Raspberry Pi, the SD card and the power source, an HDMI cable and a compatible display are needed. You will also need a USB keyboard and mouse, just like a regular computer. Wi-Fi and Bluetooth are already built into the Raspberry Pi 3 and higher models. If you are using an older version of the Raspberry Pi, you can use USB dongles for this. If you prefer Ethernet for connectivity, Ethernet ports are available on all Raspberry Pi models (except the Zero and Pico).

<u>Wireless access to the printer:</u> Maybe you still have an old printer with a USB port lying around somewhere that you would like to use wirelessly? A Raspberry Pi offers you the solution by serving as a kind of printer server. This is done by installing the Samba file sharing program and then the Common Unix Printing System (CUPS). The CUPS includes printer drivers and a management console. After installing the necessary software, configure the Raspberry Pi so that any computer on your network can access the printer. However, this only works if your printer has a USB cable. Adapters are also available as an alternative.

A retro gaming computer: The Raspberry Pi is great as a retro gaming computer, which is an often used application. The Raspberry Pi is small and powerful enough to use as a full arcade system or Game Boy kit! There are two main platforms for retro gaming: Recalbox and RetroPie. With the help of these platforms you can revive the games from your childhood.

Robot control: The Raspberry Pi offers a number of robotics solutions. For example, you could use a custom robotics package for your Raspberry Pi that runs on batteries and is used to interact with and control a robot. A Raspberry Pi Zero W is ideal for this.

Game Server: Raspberry Pi OS (Raspbian), the default operating system of the Raspberry Pi, comes with a version of Minecraft pre-installed. However, the Raspberry Pi can also be used as a Minecraft game server, so you can play from anywhere on your home network. If you use multiple Raspberry Pis, you can use one as a central server to make it a multiplayer game and play with friends.

Creating time-lapse videos: If you use the Raspberry Pi camera module with a custom script, you can record time-lapse videos with your Pi. To create such videos, frames are created with a time delay. You will need a portable power supply for this, and preferably a tripod as well.

FM radio station: Do you feel the need to share yourself with the world? Do you want to reach people who don't have internet access? In these cases, the first thing that comes to mind is the radio. How great that the Raspberry Pi can broadcast on the FM frequency band!
Before you send a message over the radio, you should consider that sending over FM without a license is illegal. By the way, the Raspberry Pi can only transmit over short distances. This can be an advantage in a remote corner of the world, but it is not ideal for use in cities. You will need a portable power supply solution and soldering skills to implement it. All audio data that you want to transmit should be loaded onto the microSD card in advance.

<u>Security system:</u> Do you value security and monitoring of your home? Then you can use the Raspberry Pi camera module to create a security camera or just a simple USB webcam. You will need a microSD card or another external USB-connected storage medium with plenty of memory to store the recordings.

<u>Web server: Setting up</u> a Raspberry Pi as a web server is another great use case. It means that the mini-PC can be set up to host a website. There are several ways to do this. First, you need to install the appropriate software, which includes Apache and its associated libraries. You could also set up a full LAMP stack, which includes PHP and MySQL in addition to Apache. However, this requires advanced knowledge or outside help. You can also install specialized web software like WordPress.

By the way, in later lessons we will have a look at some (other) projects step by step, which we will implement together in detail. So don't worry, there will be a step-by-step guide to a few beginner projects with the Raspberry Pi. But first we will have a look at the difference between the Raspberry Pi and a normal PC, and then we will learn how to set up the Raspberry Pi.

3 Raspberry Pi vs. desktop PC

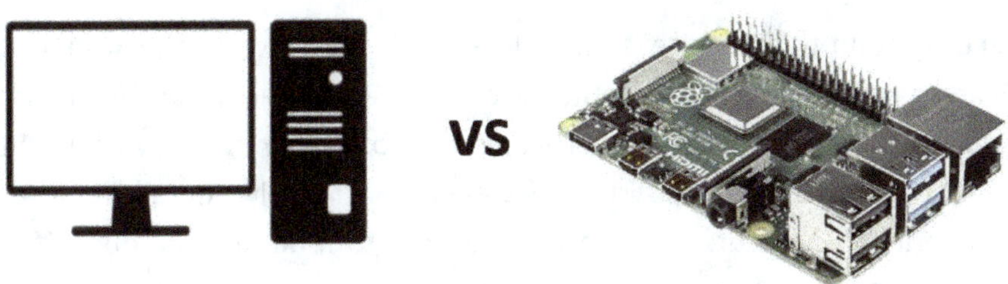

The popularity of the Raspberry Pi has grown over time, and more and more people are using this handy mini-PC. The current Raspberry Pi versions can perform most everyday activities that a normal PC can. In reality, however, there are significant differences between these two systems, which we would like to take a closer look at below.

The Raspberry Pi differs from a typical computer foremost in terms of construction, size, price, connectivity, memory, and storage. In addition, the Raspberry Pi also differs in the input/output hardware, i.e., the available connection options, storage solutions and displays.

Composition of the motherboard:

In a desktop PC, the motherboard is the foundation or base of the computer system. Other components of a normal computer are the power supply, the main memory (RAM), the hard drive, the CPU (main processor) and the GPU (graphics processor). They are connected to the motherboard via standard connections and – since they are mostly attached via plug-in connections – are replaceable or upgradable.

The circuit board of a Raspberry Pi is much smaller compared to a normal desktop computer. This means that all the essential components, such as USB ports, RAM, processor and so on, have to fit on a tiny circuit board. Since these components are soldered, replacing components or upgrading the motherboard is severely limited.

Size of the computer:

An easy point to recognize is the difference in size between the Raspberry Pi and a normal desktop computer. A desktop PC is usually the size of a file folder or a shoebox. The Raspberry Pi, on the other hand, is only about the size of a credit card. This size difference is relatively impressive when comparing the feature set of a Raspberry Pi to a desktop PC and offers various advantages for using a Raspberry Pi.

Architecture of the CPU (main processor):

As for the CPU, i.e., the main processor, a normal computer has an x86 or x64 processor. Most systems today are 64-bit systems (x64), 32-bit CPUs (x86) are becoming increasingly rare.

A Raspberry Pi is controlled by an ARM-based CPU (RISC = Reduced Instruction Set Computing). The difference between the x86 and ARM design is that in the ARM design the instruction processing is much simpler and leaner. In the x86 design (CISC = Complex Instruction Set Computing), on the other hand, more complex instruction sets can be processed, e.g., one instruction set can execute several operations.

Due to their simple design, ARM-based CPUs take up less space and have lower power requirements, making them ideal processors for small devices like the Raspberry Pi.

Computing power:

In general, the computing power of a normal computer is greater than that of the Raspberry Pi. However, for the vast majority of applications, the Raspberry Pi's computing power is considered sufficient.

Let's compare a Pentium G6400 and the Raspberry Pi 4. The price of a G6400 CPU is about $70. For that, you get a dual-core processor with hyperthreading that runs at 4 GHz. The Raspberry Pi 4, on the other hand, has a quad-core ARMv8 processor with only 1.5 GHz. However, the price of the entire Raspberry Pi 4 is less than half the price of the G6400 CPU.

Hard disk space and memory:

The Raspberry Pi computers require a microSD card as a hard drive replacement. Reading and writing on the card can be relatively slow compared to hard drives or the newer SSDs that are now widely available.

Normal microSD cards have a lifespan of 10 years. However, you may have to replace them sooner than you think because operating systems do a lot of writing and reading of the data, which shortens the life of an SD card. microSD cards of up to 1 TB (1000 GB) are no longer rare today, but they are relatively expensive. HDD or SSD hard disks of a normal desktop PC also have an average lifespan of about 10 years and a storage capacity of several TB or a few GB depending on the design, but they are significantly larger.

The Raspberry Pi 4 has up to 8 GB of working memory, which is already an astonishing amount for such a small PC. A normal PC has 8 GB, 16 GB, 32 GB or even more working memory, depending on the configuration.

Pricing:

One of the main reasons for the development of the Raspberry Pi computers was the relatively high prices for normal PCs. When the Raspberry came on the market, many students, especially in poorer regions, simply could not afford a normal desktop computer. A Raspberry Pi is available for as little as 1/10 or even 1/20 of the price of a desktop PC. A good Raspberry Pi is already available for around $50. Depending on the equipment or model, this amount can be even lower or higher, but ranges between $10 and $100. A normal PC, on the other hand, can cost between $500 and $2000.

Connectivity:

The term "connectivity" refers to the computer's ability to connect to the Internet and other devices.

The latest Raspberry Pi model has a few more ports than previous models had. It has four USB ports, one or two HDMI outputs, an audio port, an Ethernet port, and Bluetooth and Wi-Fi capabilities.

Compared to a typical computer, you might be missing some ports, like a microphone port, additional USB ports or an audio output. However, the Raspberry Pi basically has all the important ports, and everything else can be added with USB adapters or USB hubs. Besides, the trend is more towards wireless connectivity anyway. The Raspberry Pi is well-equipped for this with Bluetooth and Wi-Fi functions.

In the next chapter, we'll get started with the practical part of the course. We will first look at how to set up the Raspberry Pi for the first time. This will be followed by the operating systems you can use, how to use the most essential sensors and components and DIY projects as well as a small troubleshooting guide for a quick error analysis. Let's go!

4 Setting up the Raspberry Pi for the first time

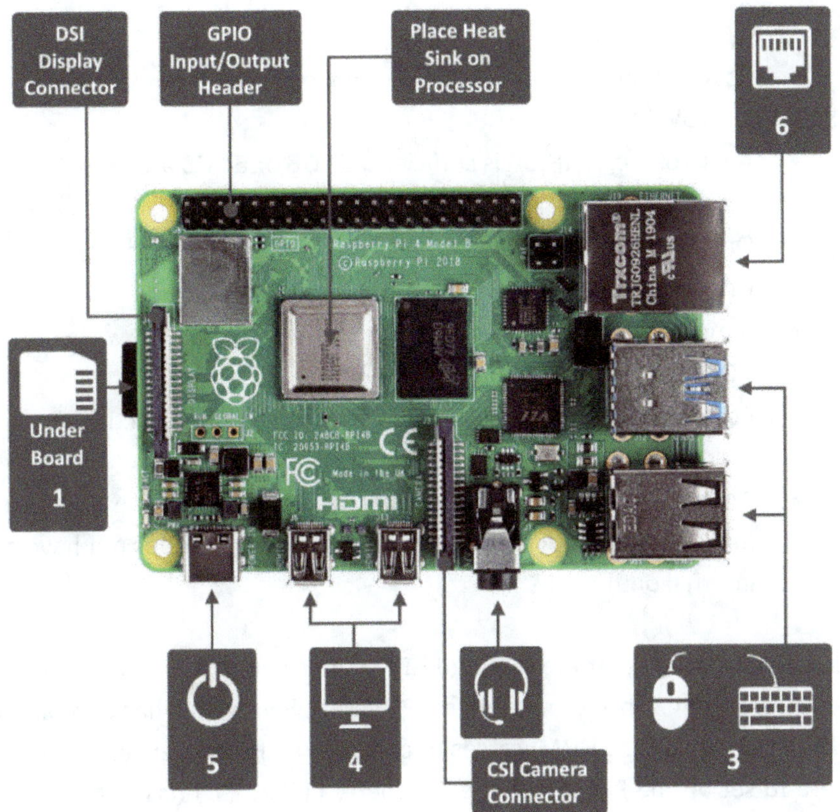

Now that you've decided to get a Raspberry Pi and use it to explore the world of computers and electronics, the first thing we need to look at is how to set up the Raspberry Pi. Setting up the Raspberry Pi requires some important components, which you can often order as a kit.

The most important thing to know before setting up a Raspberry Pi system is that not all types of devices are compatible with every Pi system. So check the compatibility before you buy parts and set up the Raspberry Pi system.

4.1 | Step 1: Required components for setup

To set up a Raspberry Pi system, you mainly need the following components:

- Power supply (depending on version, e.g., USB-C power supply with 5V 3A)
- A microSD card (8 GB is sufficient, 32 GB or 64 GB are recommended)
- One keyboard
- One mouse
- A monitor for display (you can also use a TV)
- HDMI cable
- Bag or case (not mandatory, but recommended protecting the Raspberry Pi)
- Desktop PC or notebook to prepare the microSD card as well as a micro SD reader (if your desktop PC or notebook does not have an internal one)

It should be noted that the required HDMI cable depends on the Raspberry Pi you are using. Since the Raspberry Pi Variant B Version 4 has two Micro-HDMI outputs, Micro-HDMI cables or corresponding adapters are required here to set up the Pi 4. Since the Raspberry Pi Zero (W) has a mini-HDMI port, mini-HDMI cables are required for connecting to a monitor with this variant. All other Pi models, such as the variant B version 3, have conventional HDMI ports and can be connected to a monitor or TV via them.

4.2 | Step 2: Ensuring the power supply

The Raspberry Pi Variant B Version 4 and the Raspberry Pi 400 are powered via a USB Type-C port, which requires the use of such a power supply with a voltage of 5 volts and 3 amps. At this point, it is important to note that most Type-C chargers that you can use for smartphones are <u>not suitable</u> for powering in the case of the Raspberry Pi, as they provide the appropriate voltage of 5V, but not enough amps (current) for the task. However, a USB-C laptop charger would be usable.

All other Raspberry Pi versions are powered via a micro-USB port. This means that you can use any suitable charging cable from your smartphone or use a suitable adapter for power supply. You can also power your Raspberry Pi system by connecting it to one of the USB ports of a normal PC.

The Pi systems do not have a built-in power switch, so you simply turn them on by connecting them to an external power supply. To turn them off, you could theoretically just unplug them. However, in a few cases, this can cause problems such as data loss. Therefore, you should always shut down the Raspberry Pi properly, there is a separate command for this.

4.3 | Step 3: Initialize the SD-card

We know by now that the Raspberry Pi does not have an internal hard drive storage, but an external microSD card is needed for this. On this SD card we will load and install the file of the operating system in the following step.

There are more than a dozen operating systems that you can use with the Raspberry Pi, you can even run Windows 10 on variant B version 3. Depending on the requirements and the application, a certain amount of memory is needed. Make sure you buy or use a card with at least 8 GB of storage, ideally get a card with 32 GB or more right away to have enough storage capacity. It is also recommended to format the SD card before using it with your Raspberry Pi system. Especially if you are using an SD card that you still had at home.

4.4 | Step 4: Download the operating system

Once you have all the necessary components, you can use the instructions below to install an operating system for your Raspberry Pi onto the SD card. You can do this using your desktop PC as follows. First, install the Raspberry Pi imager from the official Raspberry Pi website, which you can download here: https://www.raspberrypi.com/software/ for Windows, macOS, or

Linux. Using this software (Raspberry Pi imager), you can both download the latest version of the Raspberry Pi operating system and also install it on the SD card. There are also alternative methods, such as obtaining a Raspberry Pi OS image file, but the "imager" simplifies this process. After downloading and installing the Raspberry Pi imager on your computer, the following dialog should open on your screen.

You must then first click on the "Choose OS" button. Then another dialog box will appear on your screen. In this dialog box, you will see different options, select the recommended option, which is "Raspberry Pi OS (32-bit)" as shown.

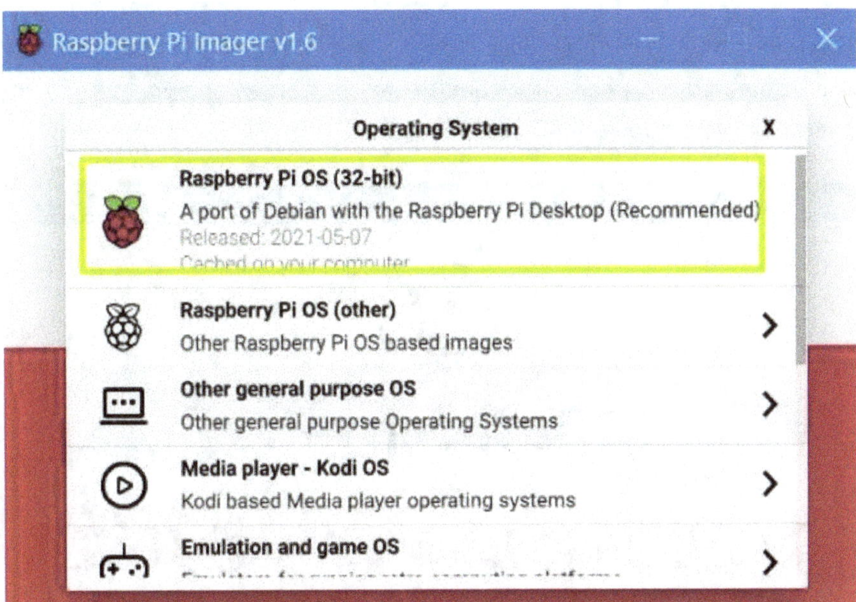

The next step is to copy the operating system file to the SD card. To do this, you must first connect the SD card to your desktop PC, using an internal or external reader.

Then select the SD card by clicking on "Choose SD Card". Once the card has been detected, you can click the "Write" button as shown to copy the operating system to your SD card.

4.5 | Step 5: Final setup steps

Your SD card now contains the latest version of the Raspberry Pi operating system. Now it is time to insert the SD card into the Raspberry Pi. To start the actual installation of the Raspberry Pi, you will need the following items.

- Raspberry Pi
- microSD card with the latest Raspberry Pi OS version
- HDMI cable and monitor
- A USB keyboard and mouse
- USB power supply

After you have completed all the previous steps and connected the devices, power up the Raspberry Pi using the power supply (charging cable) and the installation process will begin. The first time you boot up, you will most likely see a "Welcome to Raspberry Pi" dialog box that will guide you through configuring important settings.

In this dialog box, you can select your country, language and time zone. After you have made your selection, click the "Next" button.

In the next step, a username and password must now be assigned. By the way, the default username is "pi" and the default password is "raspberry".

You can change the username and password as shown.

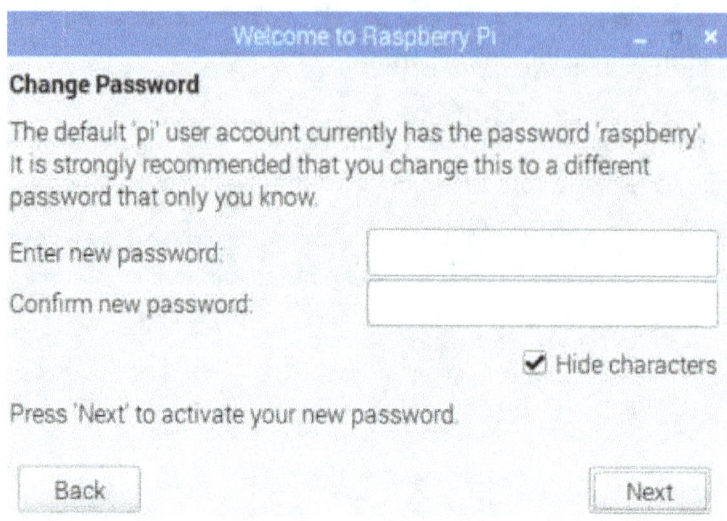

Now it is time to establish an internet connection to your Raspberry Pi. If you have a Wi-Fi connection, select it. If you want to use a LAN connection, you can skip this step with "Skip".

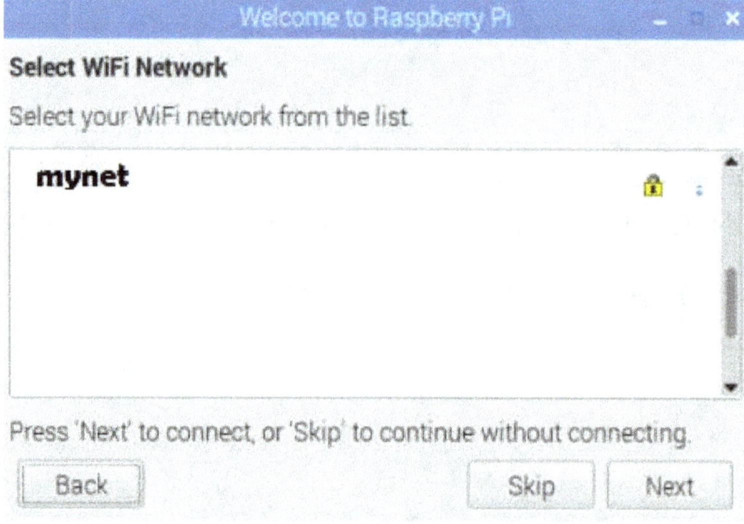

The final step in the installation process is to check for software updates. You can either select the "Next" option to check for software updates, or click "Skip" if there is no Internet connection, or you prefer not to run the process now.

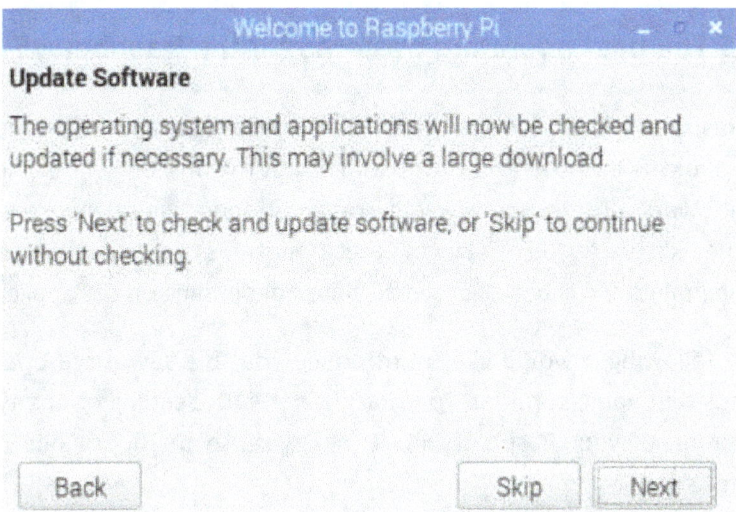

Congratulations, now you have completed all the steps and are ready to use your new Raspberry Pi system. Click the "Done" button when the installation is complete.

In the following chapter we take a look at some alternative operating systems you can use for the Raspberry Pi.

5 The best operating systems for the Raspberry Pi

The Raspberry Pi OS we just installed is the official and recommended system for the Raspberry Pi. However, it is not the only one with which the mini PC works. There is now a wide range of operating systems available for the Raspberry Pi. Each of these systems has advantages and disadvantages and is better or worse suited depending on the application.

In the following, I would like to introduce you to a few more operating systems that you can run on your Raspberry Pi. Depending on the type of application of your Raspberry Pi, it makes sense to choose one of the systems specifically.

Raspberry Pi OS (formerly Raspbian):

Raspberry Pi OS or formerly Raspbian is a Debian-based operating system (Debian is again a general-purpose operating system) designed specifically for the Raspberry Pi and is the ideal operating system for Raspberry Pi users.

Here, a number of pre-installed applications like Minecraft Pi, Java, Mathematica or Chromium are already included. Raspbian is the operating system officially recommended by the Raspberry Foundation and can do all the tasks you want to do with your Raspberry Pi system.

Open-Source Media Center (OSMC):

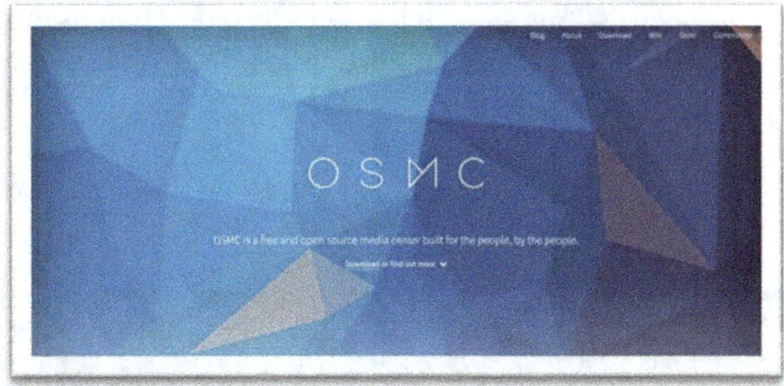

OSMC (Open-Source Media Center) is a free, open source and user-friendly as well as standalone Kodi operating system that can play almost any type of media. By the way, Kodi (formerly XMBC) is a free and cross-platform media player software.

This operating system has a modern, attractive and simple user interface and is extremely configurable thanks to the various integrated graphics. If you mainly want to manage media content on your Raspberry Pi, you should choose OSMC.

RISC operating system:

The "RISC OS" operating system is a unique open source operating system developed exclusively for ARM processors by the inventors of the original ARM. It has nothing to do with Linux or Windows and is managed by a dedicated group of volunteers. If you decide to use the RISC operating system, you should be aware that it is significantly different from any Linux or Windows operating system you have used before and will take some time to get used to.

Windows IoT Core:

Windows IoT Core is a Windows operating system designed specifically for the Raspberry Pi to serve as a development environment for programmers and developers. With the help of this system, programmers can create prototypes of IoT devices using the Raspberry Pi and Windows 10. IoT stands for Internet of Things. These are devices that are connected to a network (via WLAN or cable) and can collect, process and store data. Due to the strong networking, high efficiency can be achieved in everyday life and in industry.

The operating system focuses on security, connectivity, creativity, and cloud integration. One of its special features is that you can only use it if you have Windows 10 installed on your PC, since it requires Visual Studio on a Windows 10 configuration to work.

Retropia:

"Retropie" is a renowned operating system that turns your Raspberry Pi into a retro gaming system. It is based on the Raspberry Pi OS and allows you to revive older PC and N64 games. Retropie is easy to install and provides a user-friendly environment to launch and play your favorite games. Before you can start playing, you must first install ROMs (read-only memory) on your Raspberry Pi. ROMs are computer files that are necessary to play the old games. You can search for them online. There are also pre-installed SD cards with thousands of games sold on Amazon. It is recommended to purchase such a card before spending hours searching for games on numerous websites.

Ubuntu Core:

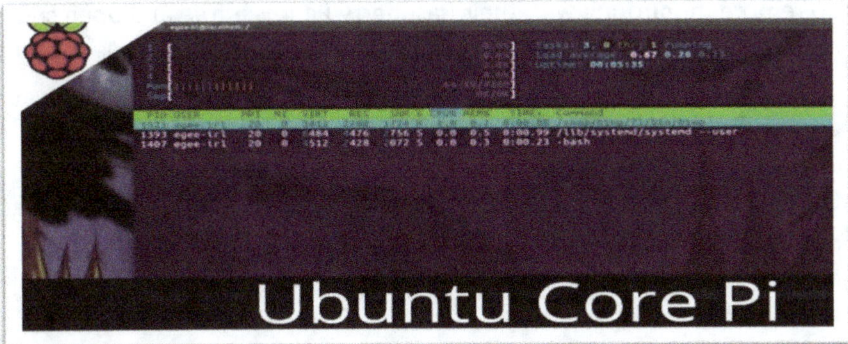

Ubuntu quickly became the world's most popular Linux-based operating system. This Debian-based operating system has a faster development cycle and offers the latest updates much earlier than Debian. If you are familiar with Ubuntu and are looking for a replacement for Raspberry Pi OS, Ubuntu is an excellent choice.

Apart from a more modern user interface, the basic programs are the same as on Raspberry Pi OS: LibreOffice, Minecraft PI, Scratch, and so on. However, there are also some minor customizations, such as Firefox as the default browser.

Domoticz OS:

The "Domoticz OS" operating system is a system for anyone who wants to do remote monitoring with their Raspberry Pi. It is a free and open source operating system for remote monitoring and control of devices like switches, cameras as well as meters like thermostat, electricity, gas, water, etc. Individual alarms can also be set up for each device.

Otherwise, self-learning sensor systems, extensive logging and compatibility with external devices are other outstanding features of Domoticz OS.

Kano OS:

"Kano OS" is an operating system specially designed for children. Kano is a company that sells computer kits for children or even schools to teach how to use a computer. After installation, a funny designed window helps you to create a user profile.

In the menu, you can also discover other applications, including the most popular apps (Minecraft and YouTube), as well as special apps for projects for kids.

6 Background knowledge - Fundamentals of electrical engineering

6.1 Introduction to electricity and digital electronics

6.1.1 Electricity

Electricity is created by electrons flowing from a place with higher potential (higher energy) to a place with lower potential (lower energy). It can be relatively well imagined through a waterfall. The water (represents the electrons) flows from the top point of the waterfall (high potential, high potential energy) to the bottom point of the waterfall (low potential, lower potential energy). The potential energy is transformed into kinetic energy during this process, that's why it "loses" this high energy state in the process (but actually this energy is transformed, as said before). Similarly, the electron wants to flow from a place with higher voltage (high potential) to a place with lower voltage (low potential).

Voltage is the unit of electrical energy "generated" by the battery. The battery or any other voltage source has two terminals. One terminal is called the negative terminal and the other terminal is called the positive terminal. At the positive terminal, the voltage potential is higher than compared to the negative side. Thus, the current flows from the positive side (plus pole) to the negative side (minus pole), considering the technical direction of current.

You can think of a battery or other power-generating source as functioning like a pump. A battery, for example, "generates" voltage or energy through an electrochemical reaction inside. This voltage or energy flows out of the positive pole in the form of electrons (these electrons symbolize the water molecules that are pumped out). In order to compensate for the "lost" electrons, the battery (similar to a suction pump) draws the same number of electrons back in through the negative pole.

6.1.2 Circuit

What is a circuit? Simply put, a circuit is an arrangement of different components with an electrically conductive connection between them. For an electrical circuit or circuit to work, you need an energy source / current source, such as a battery and a consumer, such as a light bulb, as well as connections between these two components, which are called conductors. In electrical engineering, these components are represented in a circuit or a circuit as symbols as follows:

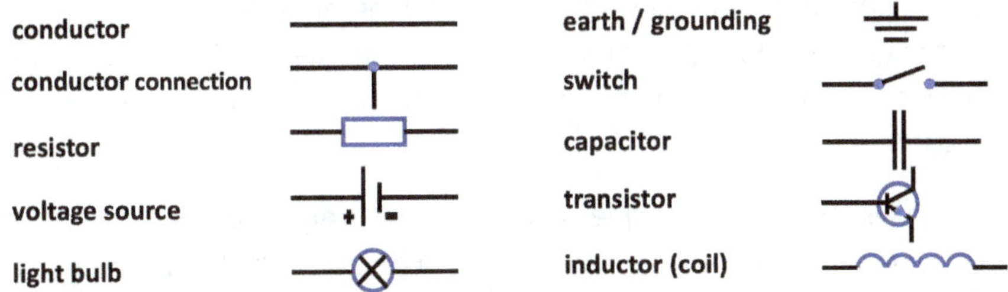

For a lamp, for example, to light up as shown in the following figure, the circuit must be closed, i.e., there must be a connection between the two poles (+ and -) of a power source (e.g., battery) and the incandescent lamp. If this is the case, current flows from one pole of the power source (e.g., battery) through the incandescent lamp and back to the other pole of the power source. When this connection is severed, e.g., by a switch, current no longer flows and the lamp no longer lights. In this case, it is called an open circuit. A short circuit occurs if the current can flow from one pole of the current source to the other pole unhindered and without first passing through an electrical component (e.g., through an uninsulated spot of a cable on a metal surface). This is because the current always takes the path of the least resistance.

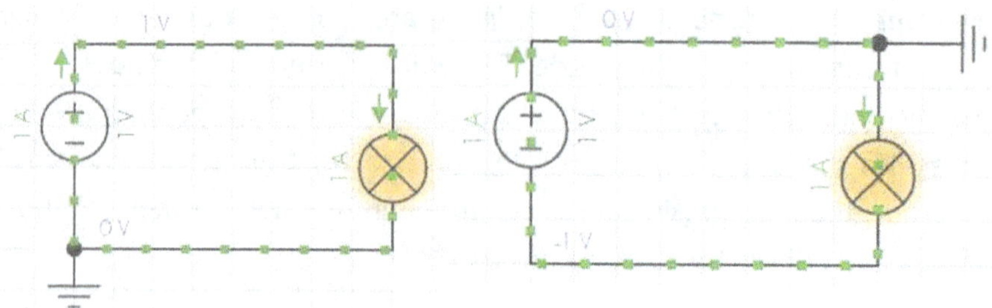

A circuit diagram is the basic concept of a circuit that can be drawn, for example, on a piece of paper or thanks to a computer program.

6.1.3 Digital electronics

In this chapter, we will also briefly look at the basics of electronics, a main area of electrical engineering. In particular, we will take a closer look at digital electronics.

The basis of digital electronics is simple switching operations. The computer is one of the best examples of these switching operations and of digital electronics. The applications that a modern computer enables us to do are achieved with the help of switching operations performed by millions of transistors.

So, what is the basic principle behind a PC? Surely, you have heard this before. It is the so-called binary system, which is based on the two numbers "0" and "1". Communication in digital systems takes place with the help of these numbers or with the help of various combinations of these two numbers.

Since the Raspberry Pi is basically nothing more than a very simple and stripped-down mini-PC, this principle is also applied here. The two binary numbers are mostly represented in today's electronic systems by the voltages 5V ("1" or HIGH value) and 0V ("0" or LOW value).

The restriction to only two numbers or voltage values seems to be very limiting, and it is very hard to imagine how a PC can achieve today's outstanding performance based on this system. However, this system and its simplicity makes sense. It simplifies the matter because it is extremely simple to recognize these two states, i.e., "0" or "1" and to definitely distinguish them from each other.

6.2 Embedded Systems (Embedded Systems)

Perhaps you have heard the term "embedded system" before. Perhaps you have also often wondered what it actually is and what it is used for.

In simple terms, an embedded system describes the presence of a chip in a technical system or on a circuit board (as in the case of the Raspberry Pi) that carries out signal transmission or data processing of input and output signals. This processing is performed by a microcontroller, which is a very small computer. This microcontroller is designed to perform certain functions and is basically nothing more than a tiny computer system consisting of a semiconductor chip.

You can program the microcontroller using PC software to perform certain operations. Actually, however, only the Raspberry Pi Pico is an "embedded system" because an "embedded system" does not have an operating system (OS) in the strict sense, as is the case with the other Raspberry Pi mini-PC models, but is programmed directly. The model series A and B of the Raspberry Pi would then have to be addressed directly without an operating system, i.e., the board's hardware with the help of other files on the SD card, in order to use the Raspberry Pi as an "embedded system".

As an example, you can see a system in the following figure, which in this case is controlled by an Arduino Uno (competitor product to the Raspberry Pi). This system switches the power of two devices (air conditioning and electric heating) depending on temperature and time. During off-peak hours (data is obtained from the utility company), it attempts to match the electricity bill with the room temperature. A budget limit for the electricity price can be set with potentiometer RV1. It also attempts to turn the air conditioner on at night and off during working hours (6 days per week). In this circuit, the temperature is measured using LM35 temperature sensor and displayed on the LCD. In this complex system, the Arduino switches the air conditioner and heater by matching the temperature, time, and power bill (three feedbacks).

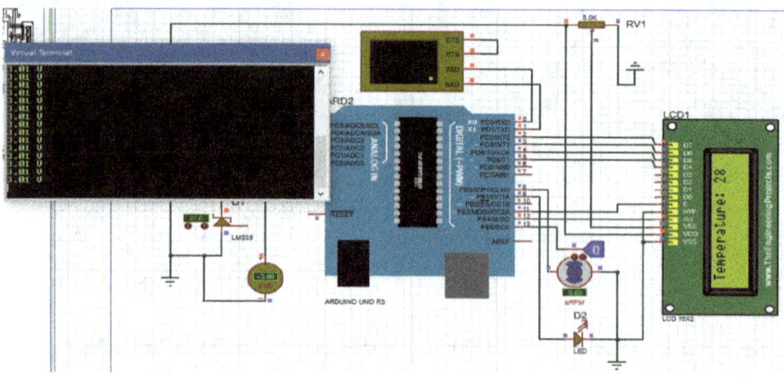

This example should only show what is possible with such a mini-PC and that even complex systems are possible.

An embedded system can be a stand-alone system, but it can also work with other systems to perform a common task. In each embedded system there are circuits that perform the functions and send or receive instructions, i.e., transmit data in the form of voltage with the help of conductive elements.

In its simplest form, an embedded system consists of the following core components: Processor, sensor, actuator and an analog-to-digital converter as well as a digital-to-analog converter. We will look at these components in a little more detail below.

Sensor:

A sensor is a component that can convert physical changes in the real world into an electrical signal that can be used by a computer or electrical system to process data. Think of it like a human's sensory organs. With the help of eyes, ears and other sensory organs, our brain can interpret the outside world and thus create an image of it. And similarly, you can imagine it with computer systems. In this example, the sensors would stand for the sense organs and the microcontroller for the brain. The electrical signals coming from the sensors to the microcontroller allow the embedded system or the microcontroller to interpret what is happening in the outside world and then execute a reaction or a program given by a programmer for a scenario by means of code.

Analog to digital converter:

Another important component of an embedded system is the analog-to-digital converter. This converts the analog signals (electrical pulses) sent by the sensors into a digital signal. For this purpose, as we already know by now, the binary system is used, i.e., the two numbers 1 and 0. These binary numbers represent the language of the system in which a microcontroller can "understand" and "react". The difference between analog and digital signals is, among other things, that an analog signal can be the carrier of several pieces of information, whereas with a digital signal, you can assign a unique piece of information to each signal. The Raspberry Pi, however, unlike the Arduino, has no analog inputs and thus no such internal converter, as we will see in the next chapter. For this, an external component must be used if analog signals, e.g., from sensors, are to be processed.

Processor:

Processors are the heart of any embedded system. A processor performs all tasks related to the received data. This component therefore receives the data, stores it, processes it and tells the system in what way it must react to this data.

Digital to analog converter:

A digital-to-analog converter is basically just the opposite of an analog-to-digital converter. It converts the digital signal sent by the microcontroller (which in turn is the response to the analog input signal converted to digital) back into an analog signal. Now why is the digital signal converted back into an analog signal? Simply because an analog signal can be understood by physical devices or actuators. The Raspberry Pi does not have such a component internally either, as already mentioned with the analog-to-digital converter.

Actuator:

An actuator (e.g., an electric motor) converts the analog signal received from the microcontroller and the digital-to-analog converter into a physical action. There are mechanical, acoustic, chemical, thermal and optical actuators that can perform physical actions in the real world according to their design. This is how embedded systems interact with the environment.

7 The most important sensors and components

The Raspberry Pi is a user-friendly single-board system that allows us to use sensors and components according to individual needs in each project. One of the outstanding features of the Raspberry Pi is the connectivity of all Arduino and Raspberry Pi sensors and components with the GPIO pins. By the way, an Arduino is a similar mini-PC that can be seen as a competitor to the Raspberry Pi. Depending on the project, you can use the sensors and components, which we will take a closer look at in this chapter, for various applications, such as weather stations, robot kits or for home automation. The big advantage to this modular design is that a Raspberry Pi system can be used to carry out a wide variety of projects by adding components or sensors.

7.1 General components and sensors

Analog sensors are devices that provide an analog output signal to the Mini PC. Analog sensors can be used to monitor changes in the environment, such as light intensity, wind speed or temperature. The output voltage varies between 0 and 5 volts for analog sensors. A voltage level of 3.5 V to 5 V is seen as a "1" signal ("on") – relating to the binary system – while a voltage level of 0 V to 3.5 V corresponds to a "0" signal ("off").

However, the Raspberry Pi has no analog input-output pins. This means that analog modules cannot be read out easily because the Raspberry Pi does not have an analog-to-digital converter (conversion of analog input signals into digital signals) or a digital-to-analog converter (conversion of digital signals into analog output signals).

A MCP3008 module is therefore necessary, for example, for the use of analog components with the Raspberry Pi.

Let's learn about some analog components and sensors that can be used in Raspberry Pi projects below.

2-axis joystick:

A 2-axis joystick has a potentiometer for each of the x- and y-axes. A certain amount of current – more or less, depending on the movement of the joystick – can flow through these potentiometers.

PIR motion sensor:

The PIR sensor is the most common motion sensor that you can use with the Raspberry Pi for various projects. The PIR sensor is a motion sensitive sensor that sends signals when an object appears in a defined area.

Inductive RFID card reader:

The RFID-RC522 is a reader. When a card comes within a few millimeters of the sensor's receiving point, a signal is sent to the Raspberry Pi. Each card has a unique code. This can be used to implement access control at doors, for example.

Gas sensor:

An MQ gas sensor is used to detect various gases at room temperature. It depends on the model of the sensor which gas types can be detected. For example, the MQ-3 gas sensor detects: ethanol, alcohol, but also smoke and some other gases.

Humidity sensor:

The measuring rod of an analog moisture sensor can be inserted into a soil and determine the moisture of the soil in this area by measuring the current flow between the measuring areas. The sensor will send a strong signal when there is more moisture in the soil. Using the Raspberry Pi, the moisture value can then be read out (MCP3008 module required).

Sensors for temperature and humidity:

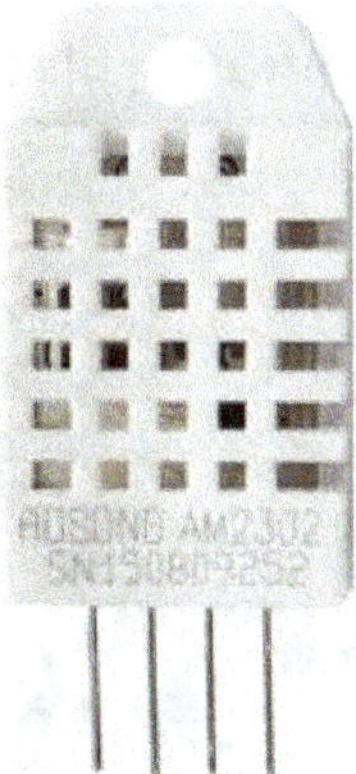

The DHT11 and DHT22 sensors can measure humidity as well as temperature. The main difference between the two types of sensors is the measuring range and accuracy. The white DHT22 can monitor humidity in a range from 0 to 100% with an accuracy of 2 percent. The blue DHT11, on the other hand, can only monitor a humidity range of 20 to 90 percent and the accuracy is slightly worse at only 5 percent.

Barometer:

The BMP180 barometer can be used to measure air pressure. In addition to this, the temperature and altitude can also be read out.

7.2 Wireless/Infrared/Bluetooth sensors

The Raspberry Pi system can also be connected to multiple wireless sensors to perform various tasks.

Bluetooth adapter:

Before the release of the Model 3, neither Bluetooth nor Wi-Fi chips were part of the Raspberry Pi board. Therefore, a Bluetooth adapter is required for data exchange with an older Raspberry Pi system.

Infrared diodes:

Most remote controls, such as for the TV, send signals via infrared LEDs. An infrared receiver can then receive these signals in turn.

433 MHz transmitter and receiver:

The 433 MHz transmitters and receivers are the most basic components for transmitting signals via radio. Because these kits are so inexpensive, they are used for a variety of tasks. For example, you can use these components to connect multiple Raspberry Pis together.

2.4 GHz module "NRF24L01+":

Using 2.4 GHz frequency is a more sophisticated way of wireless transmission. The main advantage of a 2.4 GHz transmitter over 433 MHz transmission is that a larger amount of data can be sent at once.

7.3 Components for display

As we know, the Raspberry Pi system is a modular single-board system. So, for input and output you need several kinds of devices! In the following, we will deal with a few display components that can turn the mini-PC into a full-fledged PC.

Official 7 inch Raspberry Pi touch screen:

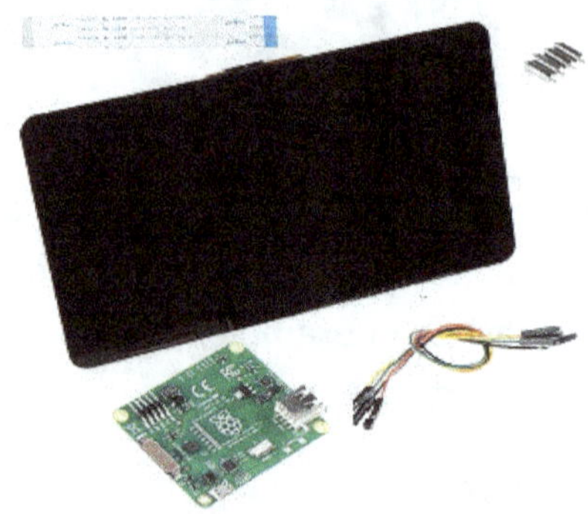

The official screen was introduced by the Raspberry Pi Foundation in September 2015. It is a capacitive touchscreen with 10 points, 7 inches and 800 x 400 pixels. A DSI connector is used for the connection between the screen and the Pi system.

3.2 inch touchscreen:

Screen sizes from 2.4 to 4.3 inches with capacitive touchscreens are also popular. Depending on the type, you can connect them either via the GPIOs or with an HDMI cable.

HD44780 display:

If you want a pure character display with a certain number of characters per line and a certain number of lines, then a HD44780 display is the best option. With a Raspberry Pi system, you can easily access such a line display.

7.4 Motors

Servo motor:

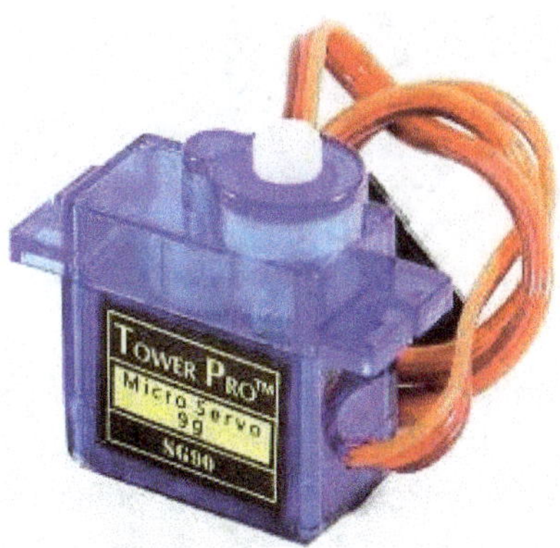

Servo motors, unlike normal motors, can be controlled by specifying a rotation angle. The motor has pulse width modulation inputs which are supported by the Raspberry Pi.

Servo Board:

It is easy to control a single servo motor with a Raspberry Pi. However, when it comes to controlling multiple servos, using the GPIOs becomes problematic. In this case, a servo driver board, e.g., "PCA9685", is an ideal solution because you can control up to 16 motors with it.

Stepper motor:

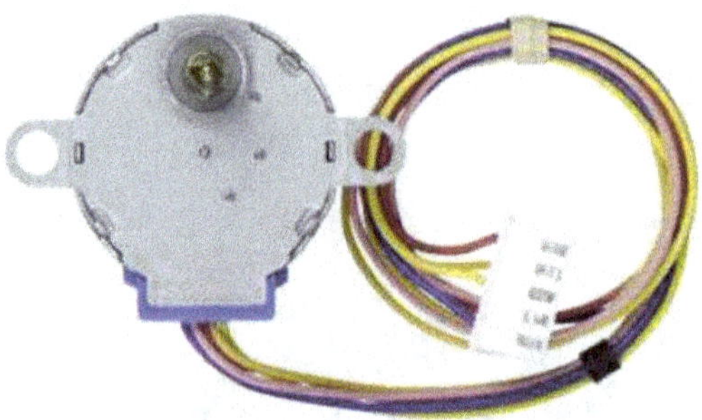

Stepper motors are electric motors that can perform a certain series of movements in a single revolution. The axis is moved between different poles by two integrated electromagnets. The polarity is described in detail in the data sheet of the motor. The type "28BYJ-48" is one of the most commonly used stepper motors.

8 Raspberry Pi DIY Projects

In this chapter, we will deal with a few DIY projects for the Raspberry Pi. For this, we will need a few electronic components, such as LEDs and resistors, and create a few program codes. However, we will not be able to learn programming in detail in this book due to complexity. You can program for the Raspberry Pi in the Python programming language. There is also a separate book from me for this that you should get if you are also interested in programming. More detailed information can be found on the last pages of this book. To program with Python, we would simply need a text editor, but it is better to use a program designed for this purpose. For example, you can use the software Thonny, which is a development environment for Python. You can download and install this software free of charge at https://thonny.org/. There is also a brief introduction and an introductory video on the website.

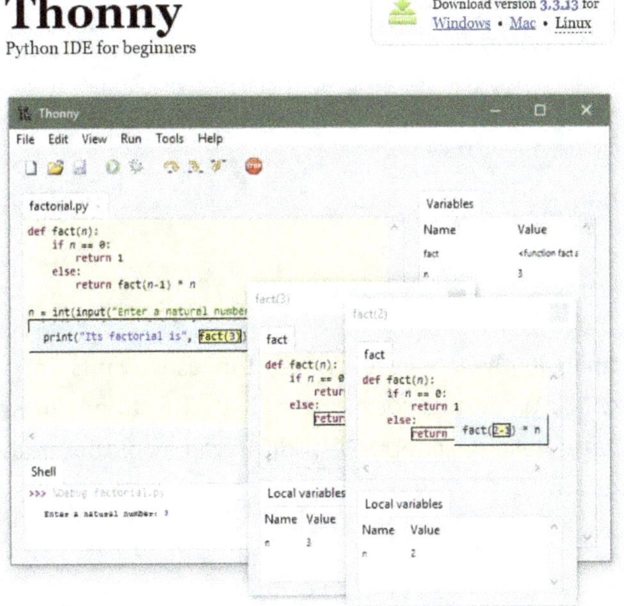

8.1 Preparation | "print" and "if" statement

In the following statement, the "print" command followed by an expression enclosed in parentheses is used. The expression to be printed is written inside the brackets.

To output any instruction with the Raspberry Pi, the following syntax must be used.

Syntax: print ("Text to be output")

Example: print ("Hello Raspberry Pi")

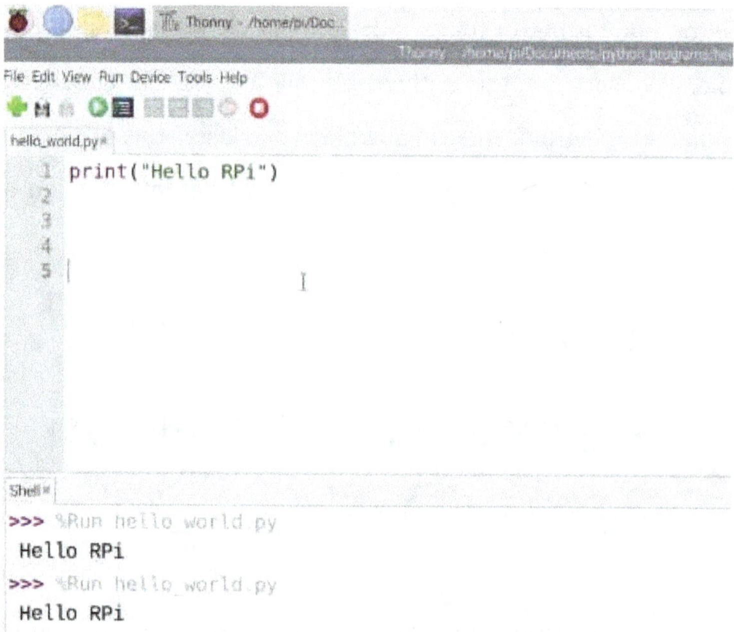

For example, in the above example, the user wants to output "Hello Raspberry Pi". When this code is compiled, the statement entered inside the brackets (Hello Raspberry Pi) is displayed as output in the console or shell monitor.

Before we start with the actual DIY projects, let's briefly look at a meaningful statement in programming, namely the if statement.

Syntax: if

In the if statement, the keyword "if" is followed by the condition that the program should check, then a colon (:) and finally the block of code that should be executed once the mentioned condition is met.

Example:

temperature =35 // *Variable "temperature" is declared and receives the value 35*

a=5 // *Variable "a" is declared and receives the value 5*

if a<=5: // *if the variable 'a' is greater/equal 5, OK is to be output*

print("OK") // *a code block that prints OK*

In the above code, first two variables were created with the number 35 for "Temperature" and with the number 5 for "a". Then a conditional statement was created which, when the variable "a" is less than or equal to 5, will display the expression "OK". If "a" exceeds 5, the "print" statement will be skipped (i.e., the word "OK" will not be printed).

8.2 Project 1 | Making an LED blink with the Raspberry Pi

Required components:

1x LED
1x 10k ohm resistor
1x Raspberry Pi
1x breadboard

The following schematic shows how to connect the LED to the Raspberry Pi board.

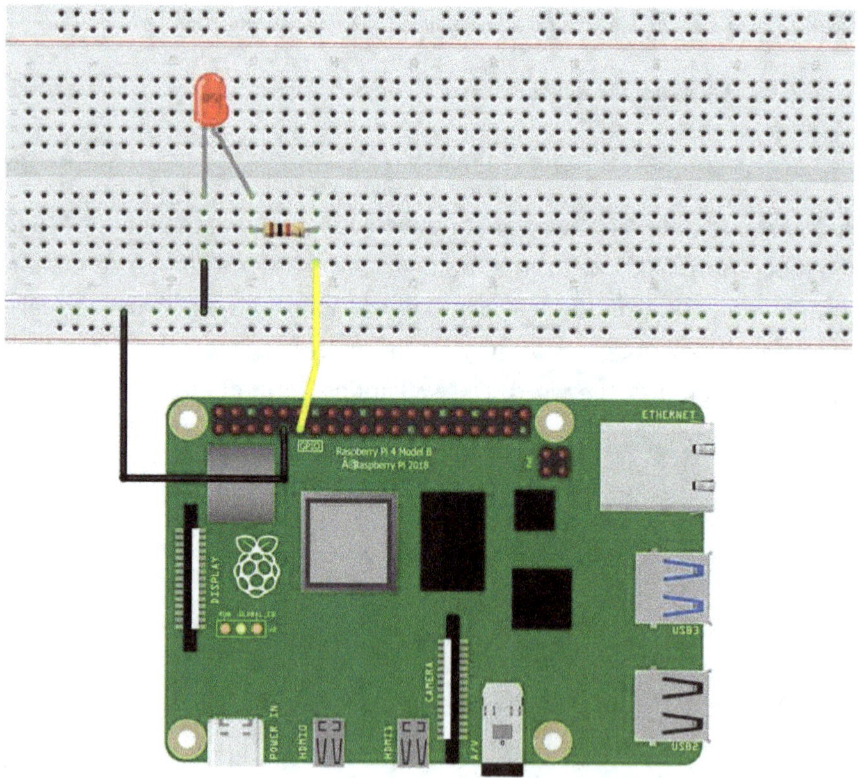

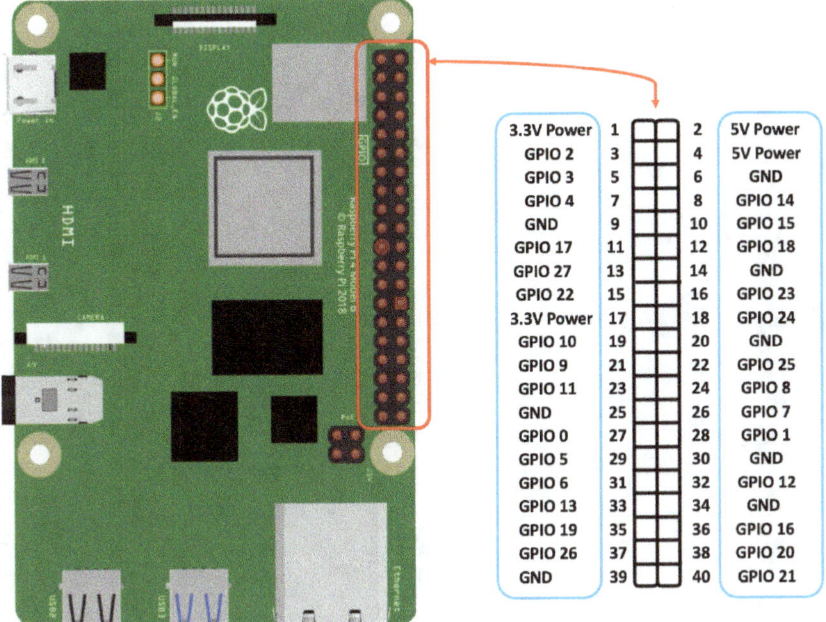

Explanation of the circuit diagram:

In this circuit, the LED cathode is connected to the GND pin of the Raspberry Pi and a resistor is connected to the anode of the LED. This resistor is called a pull-up resistor because when the turn-on signal is sent from the Raspberry Pi to the LED, the LED turns on and when the turn-off signal is sent from the Raspberry Pi, the LED turns off.

Program code:

Below is the code both pictorially and in text form.

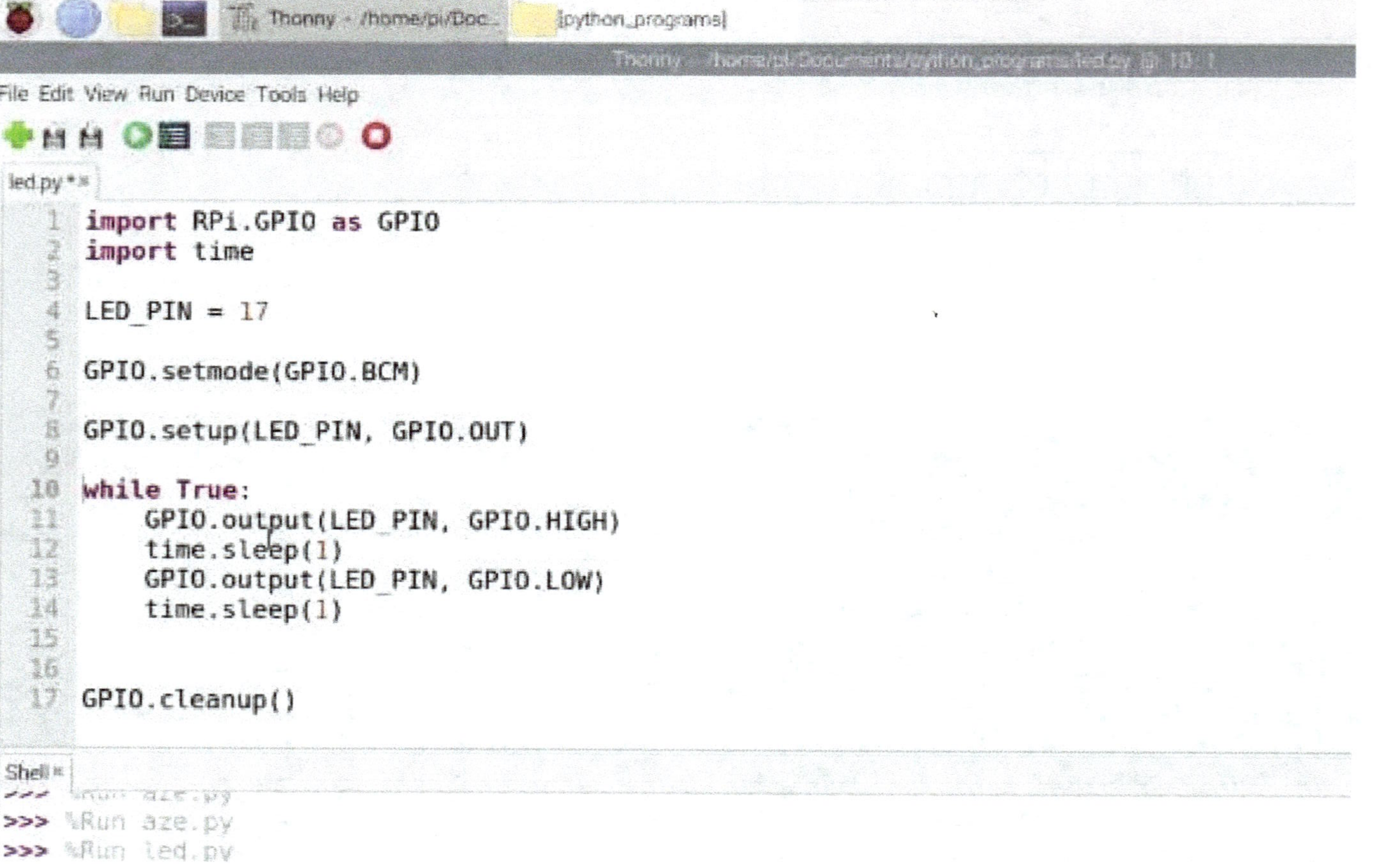
Thonny - /home/pi/Doc...   [python_programs]
Thonny - /home/pi/Documents/python_programs/led.py @ 10 : 1
File Edit View Run Device Tools Help
led.py *
1 import RPi.GPIO as GPIO
2 import time
3
4 LED_PIN = 17
5
6 GPIO.setmode(GPIO.BCM)
7
8 GPIO.setup(LED_PIN, GPIO.OUT)
9
10 while True:
11   GPIO.output(LED_PIN, GPIO.HIGH)
12   time.sleep(1)
13   GPIO.output(LED_PIN, GPIO.LOW)
14   time.sleep(1)
15
16
17 GPIO.cleanup()
Shell
>>> %Run aze.py
>>> %Run aze.py
>>> %Run led.py

```python
import RPi.GPIO as GPIO

import time

LED_PIN = 17

GPIO.setmode(GPIO.BCM)

GPIO.setup(LED_PIN, GPIO.OUT)

while True:

  GPIO.output(LED_PIN, GPIO.HIGH)

  time.sleep(1)

  GPIO.output(LED_PIN, GPIO.LOW)

  time.sleep(1)

GPIO.cleanup()
```

Explanation of the program code:

In this code, the function "RPI.GPIO" was imported from the library of the Raspberry Pi. It is a header file that is used to control the digital pins of the Raspberry Pi. Moreover, a time function "time" was used to integrate a delay. Thereafter, a variable named "LED_pin" was declared, and it was assigned the number 17 (because it is the 17th GPIO pin of the Raspberry Pi). With "GPIO.setup(LED_PIN, GPIO.OUT) " it is defined that pin 17 should be used as OUTPUT pin, i.e., PIN 17 should supply 3.3 volts to the LED. Then a WHILE loop was created, which supplies current to the LED with "GPIO.HIGH", then waits a short time with "time.sleep" and interrupts the current again with "GPIO.LOW". This process can then be perceived by us as blinking.

8.3 Project 3 | Connecting a push button to the Raspberry Pi

Required components:

1x LED
3x 10k ohm resistor
1x pushbutton
1x Raspberry Pi
1x breadboard

The following schematic shows how to connect the LED and the button to the Raspberry Pi board.

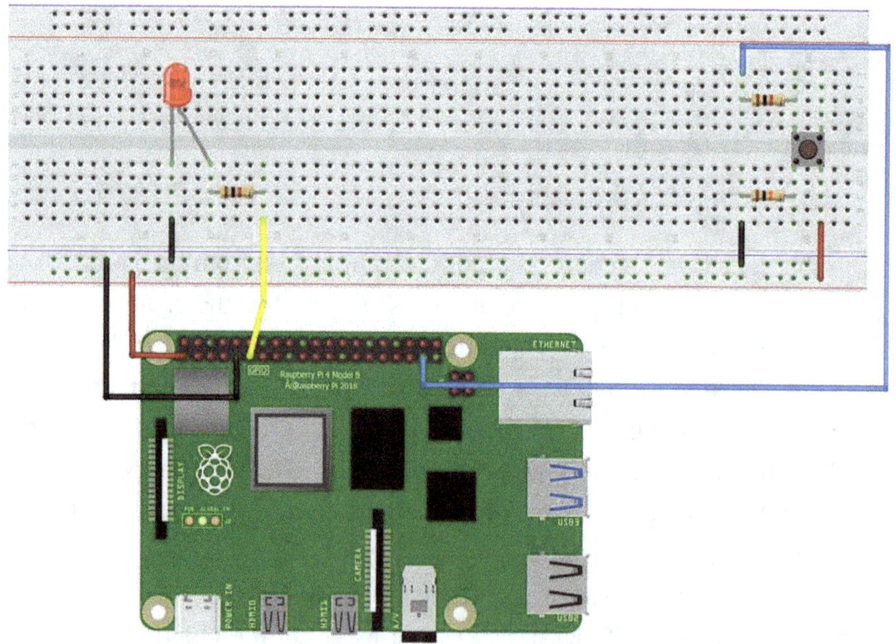

Explanation of the circuit diagram:

In this circuit, the LED and the push button are connected to the Raspberry Pi. The cathode of the LED is connected to the GND pin of the Raspberry Pi and one resistor is connected to the anode of the LED and two resistors are connected to the push button.

Program code:

Below is the code both pictorially and in text form.

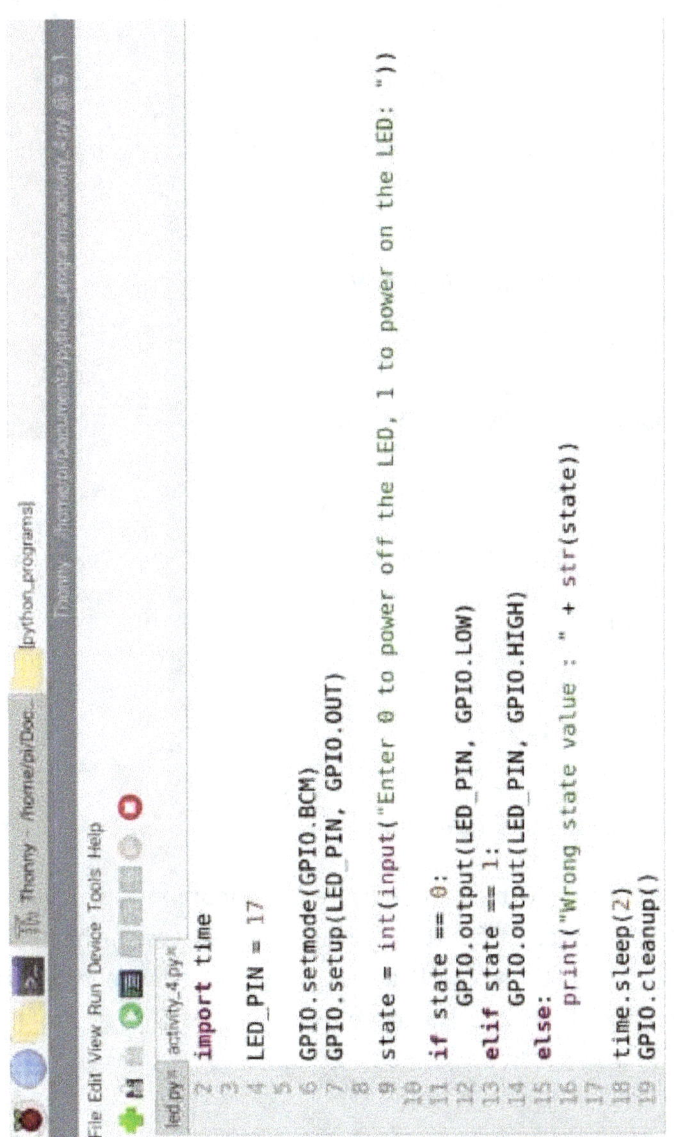

```python
import RPi.GPIO as GPIO

import time

LED_PIN = 17

GPIO.setmode(GPIO.BCM)

GPIO.setup(LED_PIN, GPIO.OUT)

state = int(input("Enter 0 to power off the LED, 1 to power on the LED: "))

if state == 0:

    GPIO.output(LED_PIN, GPIO.LOW)

elif state == 1:

    GPIO.output(LED_PIN, GPIO.HIGH)

else:

    print("Wrong state value : " + str(state))

time.sleep(2)

GPIO.cleanup()
```

Explanation of the program code:

As soon as the GPIO pins are activated, a condition is executed. If a "0" signal is transmitted when the pushbutton is pressed, the LED is to be switched off. However, if a "1" signal is transmitted when the pushbutton is pressed, the LED is to be switched on.

8.4 Project 4 | Motion detector with PIR sensor

Required components:

3x LED
1x PIR sensor
6x 10k ohm resistor
1x pushbutton
1x Raspberry Pi
1x breadboard / plug-in board

The following circuit diagram shows how to connect the components.

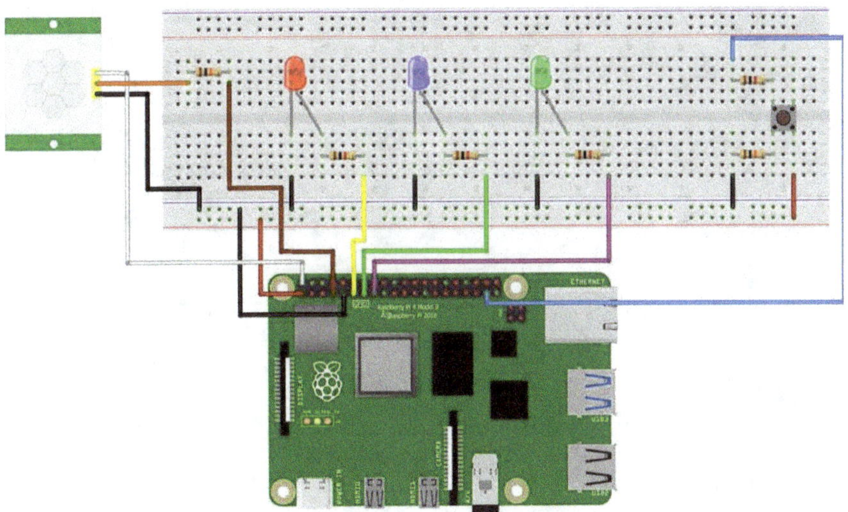

Program code:

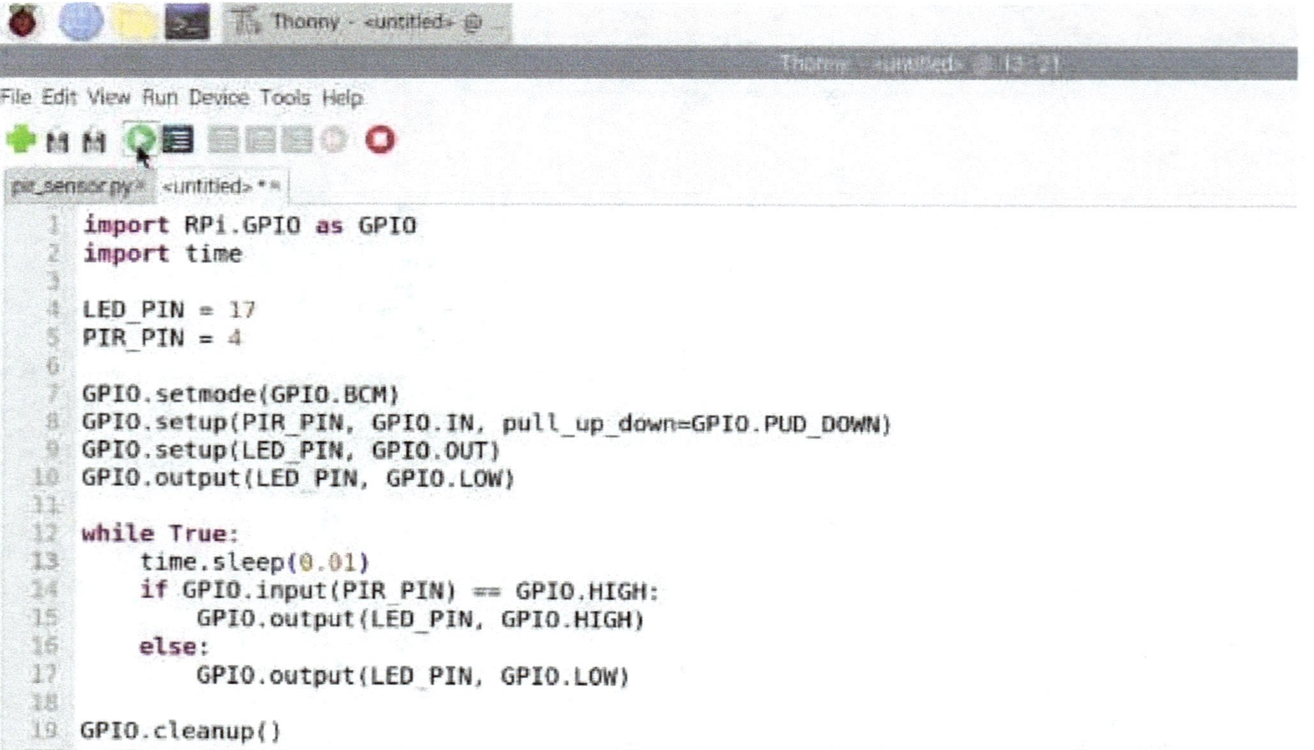


```python
import RPi.GPIO as GPIO
import time

LED_PIN = 17
PIR_PIN = 4

GPIO.setmode(GPIO.BCM)
GPIO.setup(PIR_PIN, GPIO.IN, pull_up_down=GPIO.PUD_DOWN)
GPIO.setup(LED_PIN, GPIO.OUT)
GPIO.output(LED_PIN, GPIO.LOW)

while True:
    time.sleep(0.01)
    if GPIO.input(PIR_PIN) == GPIO.HIGH:
        GPIO.output(LED_PIN, GPIO.HIGH)
    else:
        GPIO.output(LED_PIN, GPIO.LOW)

GPIO.cleanup()
```

```python
import RPi.GPIO as GPIO

import time

LED_PIN = 17

PIR_PIN = 4

GPIO.setmode(GPIO.BCM)

GPIO.setup(PIR_PIN, GPIO.IN, pull_up_down=GPIO.PUD_DOWN)

GPIO.setup(LED_PIN, GPIO.OUT)

GPIO.output(LED_PIN, GPIO.LOW)

while True:

    time.sleep(0.01)

    if GPIO.input(PIR_PIN) == GPIO.HIGH:

        GPIO.output(LED_PIN, GPIO.HIGH)

    else:

        GPIO.output(LED_PIN, GPIO.LOW)

GPIO.cleanup()
```

Explanation of the program code:

The PIR sensor used here detects human movement. When we hold our hand in front of the PIR sensor, the sensor detects the heat radiation of the hand and sends a "1" signal to the Raspberry Pi. When the signal is received, the LED on the Raspberry Pi will light up. However, the Raspberry Pi will not receive a signal if the hand is very far away from the sensor, or there is nothing in the range of the sensor at all. In this case, the LED remains off.

9 Raspberry Pi – Troubleshooting

The probability of encountering a problem with the Raspberry Pi is minimal due to its ease of use and small size. However, if something does not work, or you get stuck, you can get some advice in this chapter. Most Raspberry Pi issues are simple and can be solved in a few minutes, so don't worry! However, a few issues may take some time and expertise. In such more complicated cases, you can search for your individual problem in a forum – e.g. this one: https://forums.raspberrypi.com/ – and ask experienced users for advice.

9.1 Boot problem

The boot problem is one of the most common problems with Raspberry Pi systems. This can be caused by a variety of circumstances. A first sign for a boot problem is: The red LED (power LED) is on, but the green LED is either off or permanently on.

If your Raspberry Pi system has the same problem, then take a look at the following solution.

Problem description and solution: The green light of your Raspberry Pi indicates activity. If the light flashes at regular intervals, everything is fine with. If the light is not blinking, your Raspberry Pi has a boot issue. In this case, the first thing you should do is check the microSD card and the slot because the SD card contains the operating system or software of your Raspberry Pi. Check that the SD card is inserted correctly and that the slot is working properly. Furthermore, make sure that the operating system is properly loaded onto the SD card and that the operating system file is not corrupted.

A simple solution is to remove the SD card, format it and install the latest version of the Raspberry Pi operating system on it. Attention: If you want to keep the previous data of your SD card, copy it to another storage medium before formatting the SD card. If it still doesn't work, you can also try another SD card once. It is possible that your card is damaged. Alternatively, you can also try another operating system once if the system hangs at startup.

9.2 The Raspberry Pi turns off intermittently

With this problem, you can observe that the Raspberry Pi restarts itself at irregular intervals. In some cases, the power LED is off even if the board is powered on.

Solution: This is probably a power supply problem. For example, the Raspberry Pi 3 requires a 5 V, 2.5 A power source to function properly; any low-powered power supply will affect functionality. Check that you are supplying the Mini-PC with enough voltage (V) and, more importantly, enough current (A) if you encounter this error.

9.3 USB does not work

This issue manifests itself by USB devices connected to the Raspberry Pi either not being recognized or not working properly.

Solution: This error can occur for a variety of reasons. For example, your Raspberry Pi may not be receiving enough power (A) and therefore cannot start the USB device. However, your USB device may also be defective; in this case, test the function of the USB device with another PC first. Sometimes it also helps if you already connect the USB device to the Raspberry Pi before you turn it on.

Likewise, It is possible that the connection between your Raspberry Pi and a USB device is good, but it is not possible to operate the device. Run the following command to test if this is the case:

"isusb -t"

This command shows you the list of connected USB devices.

USB compatibility is also essential for proper interaction between USB device and Raspberry Pi. Check the compatibility and also the version of the Raspberry Pi software.

9.4 Keyboard display error

When the key shown on the display differs from the key typed on the keyboard, the error is called a keyboard display error. This problem is often caused by the default keyboard setting of the Raspbian and NOOBS software for the UK.

Solution: To solve this problem, you need to adjust the settings to your keyboard or language. This can be accomplished by navigating to the Raspberry Pi's configuration menu, then selecting the Internationalization menu, then the Keyboard Settings menu, and then scrolling down to select the keyboard style that corresponds to your keyboard's country of origin or language version.

9.5 The Raspberry Pi system does not work with an HDMI-based display

In such a scenario, your Raspberry Pi system will not work with an HDMI display.

Solution: There are two ways to fix this problem. First: Make sure you have a working HDMI cable. Second, before turning on your Raspberry Pi, connect the monitor and select the correct mode (HDMI instead of VGA). Moreover, before turning on the Raspberry Pi, make sure your monitor is powered and turned on.

9.6 Password reset error

In such a scenario, the attempt to reset the password of the Raspberry Pi is unsuccessful or the system hangs.

Solution: This is one of the signs that the Raspberry Pi is not getting enough power from the connected power source or that the power supply is fluctuating. Change the power supply of the Raspberry Pi or connect it to another power port.

9.7 Wi-Fi does not work

Wi-Fi connectivity is disabled by default when an Ethernet cable is connected to the Raspberry Pi. This was most likely added as a security measure to prevent networking between the Wi-Fi and the Ethernet port of the Raspberry Pi. So, opt for either Wi-Fi or Ethernet. If you need both, try the following solution.

Solution: To fix this problem, you can run the following command:

"Sudo update-rc networking disable"

or

"Sudo apt-get purge ifpluged"

Then you can use both network options at the same time. One thing to keep in mind is that the Raspberry Pi now works like a router, which can be a security risk.

Closing words

Excellent!

You've done it, you've worked through the beginner course.

Congratulations

In this book, I have endeavored to give you the basic knowledge for the use of a Raspberry Pi simply explained closer. I hope that I have succeeded to some extent and that this book has brought you a well understandable and practical introduction to the world of the mini-PC!

The goal of this book was to give you both theoretical background knowledge about the Raspberry Pi and an understanding of how to use the Raspberry Pi in practice.

With this basic course, you should now know everything you need to know about using a Raspberry Pi as a beginner! Of course, it makes sense not to stop at this point and rather look into an advanced book to learn even more about creating systems using a Raspberry Pi.

Together we have accomplished quite a bit in this course! Be justifiably proud of yourself if you made it to the end!

If you enjoyed this book, I would be very happy if you leave me a rating and short feedback, as well as recommend the book! Thank you very much.

If you are also interested in other books of mine on similar topics, be sure to take another look at the next pages.

Thank you very much!

Books on topics you might also like

All books are available online on the usual sales platforms. It's best to just search for the title, or feel free to visit my author page. Some of the books may not be published yet and will be released or found soon. Take a look at the books of your choice and your copy as e-book or paperback!

3D Printing:

CAD, FEM, CAM (3D Object Creation, Design, Simulation):

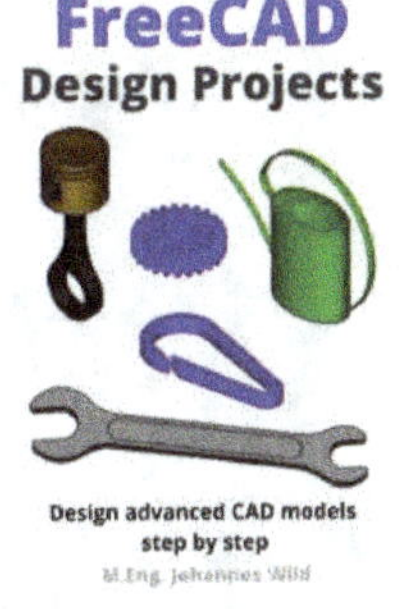

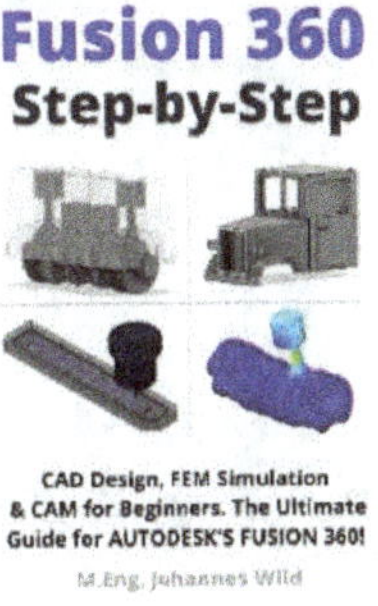

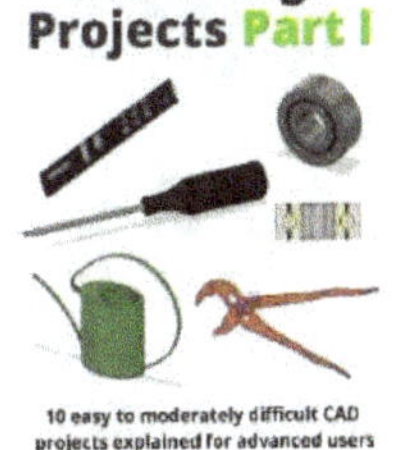

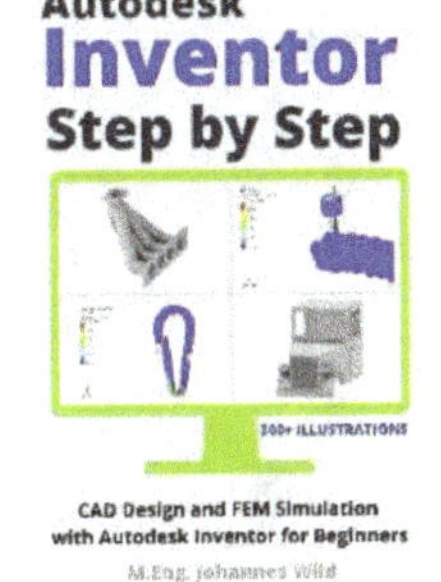

Electrical Engineering:

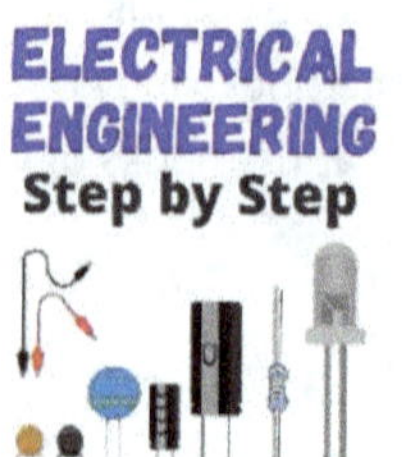

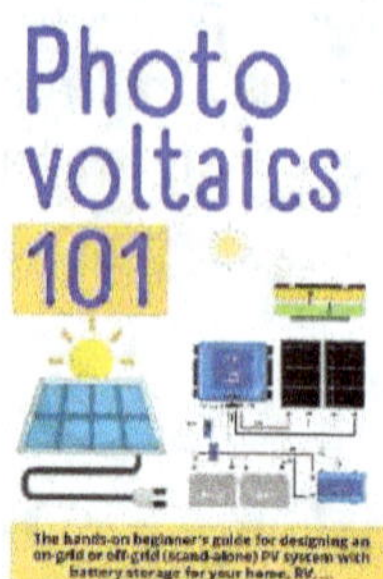

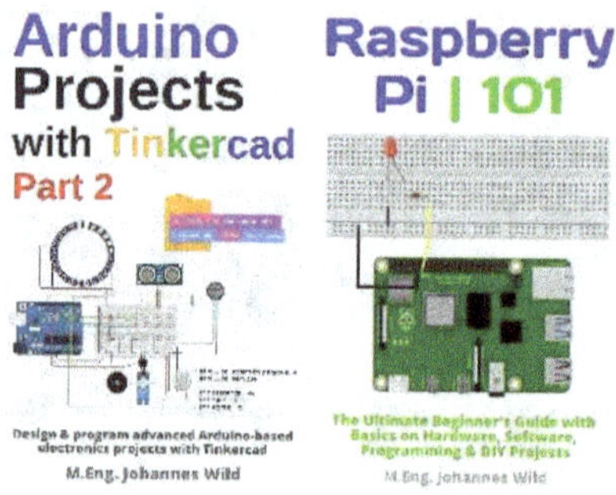

Programming and other Software:

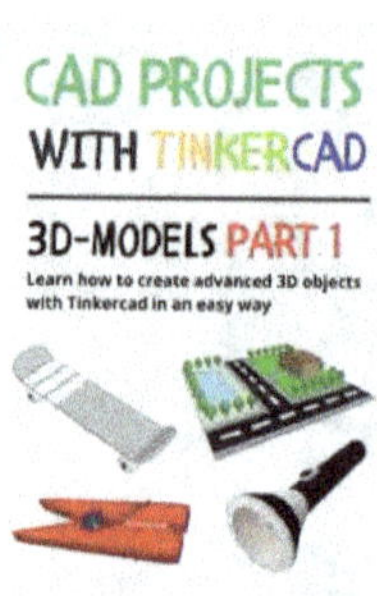

There are also identical video courses for some of these books:

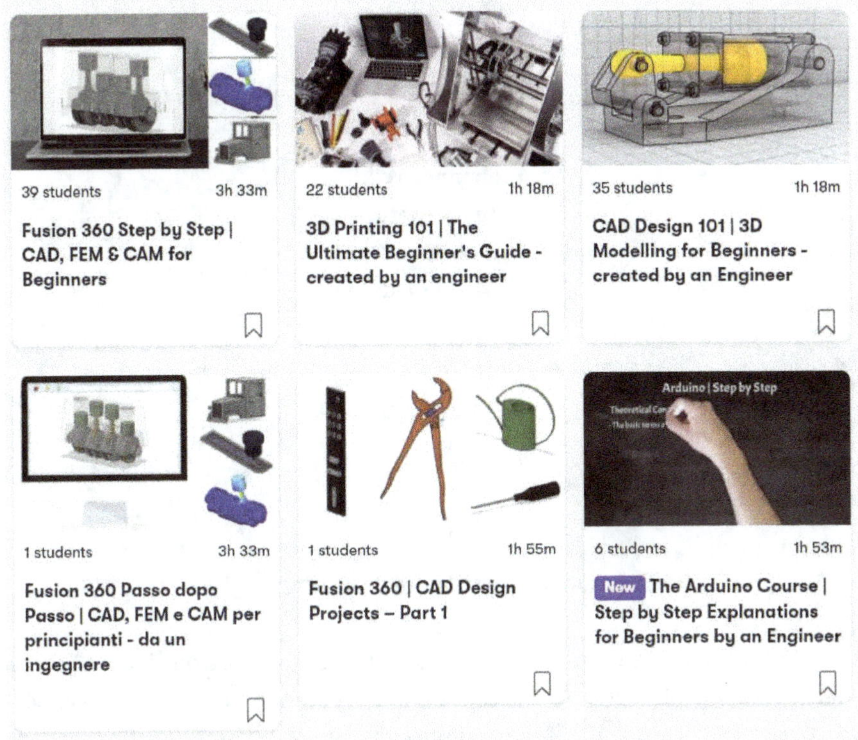

They are hosted on the learning website: skillshare.com

Be sure to use my following friends & family referral link to get a month of membership for free !

(I will get a little bonus if you choose to stay, so we will be both happy. Thanks in advance!)

https://www.skillshare.com/r/profile/Johannes-Wild/854541251

It is best to copy the link in your browser to access the free month !

Sign up today and deepen your knowledge!

Imprint of the author / publisher

© 2023

Johannes Wild
c/o RA Matutis
Berliner Straße 57
14467 Potsdam
Germany

Email: 3dtech@gmx.de

This work is protected by copyright

www.ingramcontent.com/pod-product-compliance
Lightning Source LLC
LaVergne TN
LVHW021321200726
843509LV00002B/88